For my very own Grandfather Owl.
And for anyone who has ever had to tell a story to make themselves feel at home.

- Marchella Ward

To Velle, for everything.

- Sander Berg

ADVISORY NOTE
Some content may not be suitable for younger children.

This paperback edition published in 2026 by Flying Eye Books Ltd.
First edition published in 2020 by Flying Eye Books Ltd.
27 Westgate Street, London, E8 3RL, UK
www.flyingeyebooks.com

Represented by: Abrams & Chronicle Books c/o Media Participations
57 rue Gaston Tessier, CS 50061, 75166 Paris Cedex 19, France

www.media-participations.com/en/subsidiaries
productsafety@abramsandchronicle.co.uk

1 3 5 7 9 10 8 6 4 2

Published in the US by Flying Eye Books Ltd.
Printed in China on FSC® certified paper.
ISBN: 978-1-83874-356-7

FSC www.fsc.org
MIX
Paper | Supporting responsible forestry
FSC® C137217

A JOURNEY THROUGH GREEK MYTHS

MARCHELLA WARD

SANDER BERG

FLYING EYE BOOKS

CONTENTS

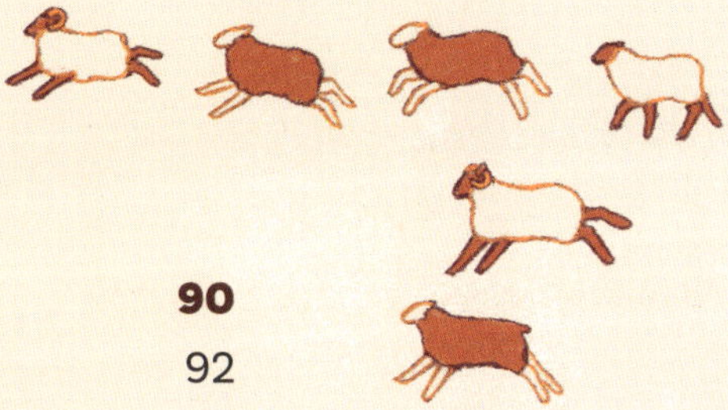

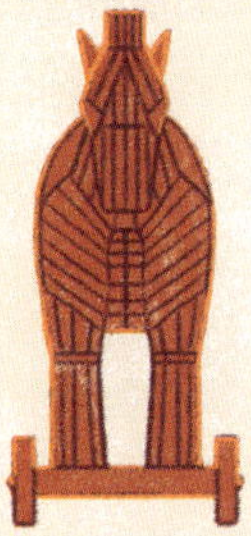

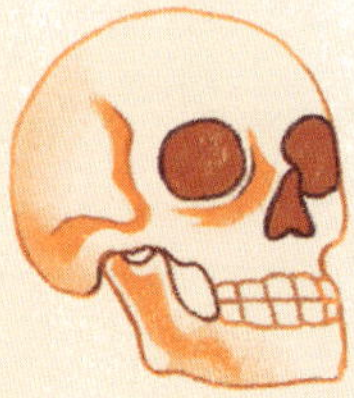

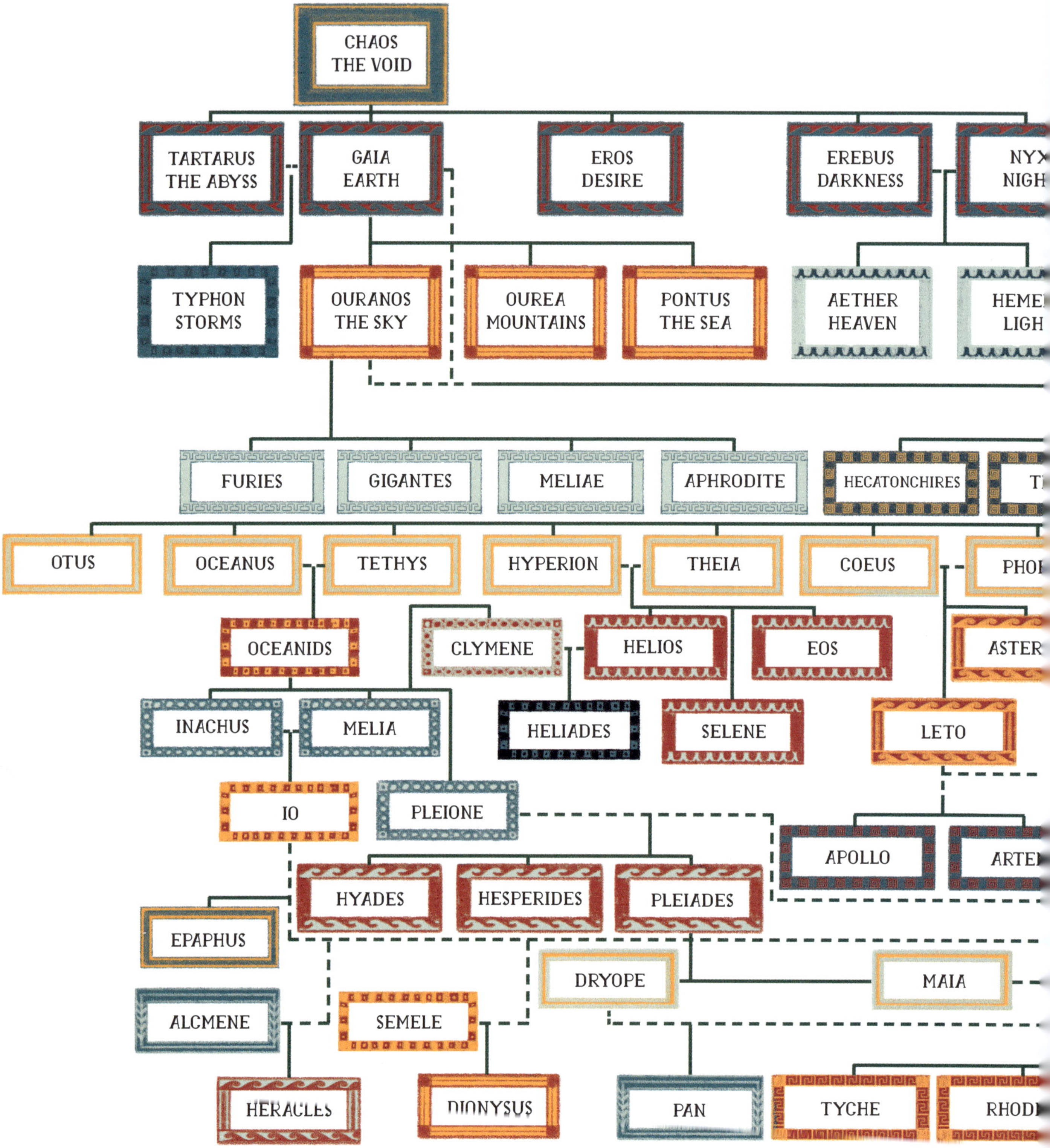
CHAOS
THE VOID
TARTARUS
THE ABYSS
GAIA
EARTH
EROS
DESIRE
EREBUS
DARKNESS
NY
NIGH
TYPHON
STORMS
OURANOS
THE SKY
OUREA
MOUNTAINS
PONTUS
THE SEA
AETHER
HEAVEN
HEME
LIGH
FURIES
GIGANTES
MELIAE
APHRODITE
HECATONCHIRES
T
OTUS
OCEANUS
TETHYS
HYPERION
THEIA
COEUS
PHO
OCEANIDS
CLYMENE
HELIOS
EOS
ASTER
INACHUS
MELIA
HELIADES
SELENE
LETO
IO
PLEIONE
APOLLO
ARTE
HYADES
HESPERIDES
PLEIADES
EPAPHUS
DRYOPE
MAIA
ALCMENE
SEMELE
HERACLES
DIONYSUS
PAN
TYCHE
RHOD

FAMILY TREE OF THE GODS AND HEROES

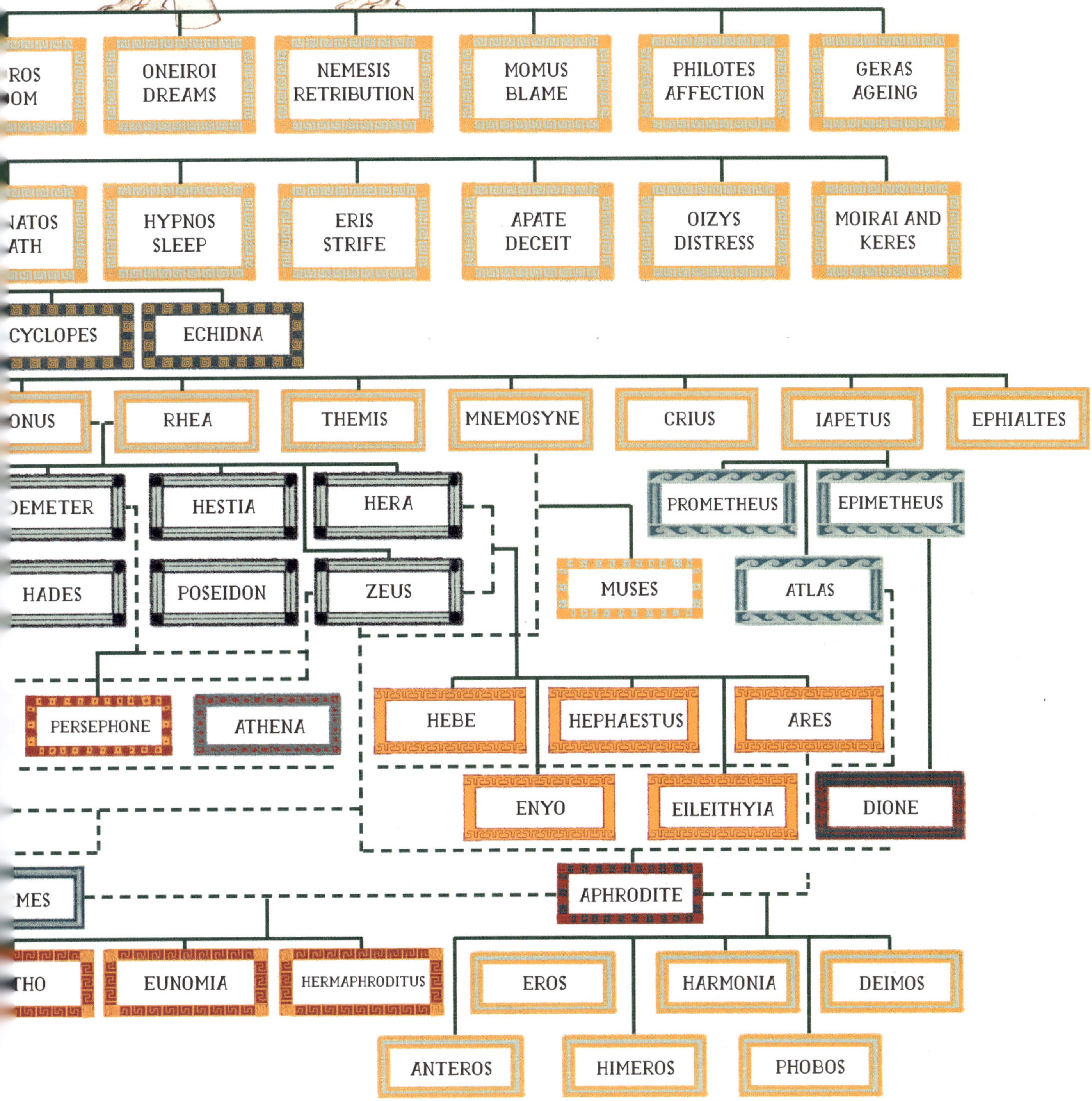

OLYMPUS
PELION
PARNASSUS
DELPHI
THEBES
ITHACA
ATHENS
OLYMPIA
ARGOS
THE UNDERWORLD
THALASSA
SPARTA
CRETE

ATHENS

Little Owl extended her talons, braced her wings against the warm wind and landed on the very top of the Parthenon. The temple looked out from the highest point of the city of Athens. Slowly, the small owl turned her head all the way around. She could see the ships docked in the port of Piraeus and the distant islands bobbing up and down on the sea. The sun was slowly setting behind the Peloponnesian mountains. Little Owl could make out the shadows of men stoking up fires for the night in the temple of Hephaistos, and the marble cheeks of the Caryatids. These statues were once women but had been turned to stone and condemned to support the weight of a temple roof on their heads for the rest of time. From the roof of the Parthenon she spotted a young magpie scratching around in the dust on the Areopagus, a huge rock sacred to the god Ares, the goddess Athena's brother.

Little Owl heard a noisy beating of wings above her and lifted her yellow eyes upwards towards the familiar sound. Her grandfather, Night Owl, landed clumsily beside her.

"You're not thinking of going down to catch that magpie, are you?" he teased. "How would you carry it all the way back up here?"

Little Owl ruffled her feathers, but was thrilled at her grandfather's arrival. "Actually, I was thinking about Athens," she said. "About how big the city is, and how many different types of people live in it. And about how lucky we are that Athena gave the owls the opportunity to sit up here and see all of it."

Night Owl tilted his head to the side, surprised by his granddaughter's sudden interest in her place in the world.

Little Owl looked at her grandfather and blinked. "What is a myth?" she asked.

Night Owl wasn't sure how to answer that question. "A myth is something that can be told," he said.

"Like a story?" Little Owl replied.

"Like a story that tells us who we are," he said. "A story that is true. Or could be true."

Little Owl looked puzzled. "You mean like a legend?"

Her grandfather paused for a moment. "When humans in the future pull coins out of the fountains of Athens and look at them," he said, "they will see owls with shining eyes staring back at them. They will tell stories about those owls and the adventures that they went on. Those stories will be legends, because they are based on real life. On history." Night Owl waited for Little Owl to take this in. "Myths are not concerned with history," he continued, "Myths are concerned with truths, or things that could be true."

Little Owl felt even more confused, though she didn't like to admit it. "So, is Athena a myth?" she asked.

Night Owl thought carefully. For as long as he could remember, owls had shared a special relationship with Athena, the goddess of war and wisdom and founder of the city of Athens.

"Oh no!" he said, and he chuckled quietly to himself. "Athena is very, very real. Or at least," he paused, "she could be."

"Owls haven't always lived in Athens, you know," Night Owl went on.

Little Owl's yellow eyes widened in surprise. Athens wasn't just her home, it was where she felt the owls had always belonged. Little Owl pleaded with her grandfather to tell her the story. He decided to start at the beginning, though his beginning was not the same place where humans liked to start their stories. In their stories, Zeus and Athena and all of the other gods who lived on Mount Olympus had always existed. The owls knew differently. In the stories of owls there was a world before humans, before the gods and before Athens. Before even the owls themselves. It was these stories that had taught the owls all of their wisdom, and it was here that he had to begin. Night Owl glanced at the twilight sky. It would soon be dark, and he had a busy night of hunting mice for his family to eat ahead of him.

Nevertheless, he began...

THE BEGINNING OF THE WORLD

Long ago, before earth, sea and land existed, the whole world looked the same. It was an enormous mist made up of tiny pieces of everything all muddled up together. At that time it had no name, but the Greeks called it 'Chaos'. No words could describe it: it was both warm and cold, light and dark, divine and human, wet and dry at the same time. Somehow - no one knows quite how - Chaos was tamed. The Earth was squeezed out of the sea and sifted out of the sky. Some say that it was Chronos, the god of time, who disentangled the elements and gave them each a name and a place, but others say that he did not yet exist. When everything had been fixed in its place, constellations of stars began to shine in the sky, and the sea began to flow up towards the shore and back out again, setting a daily rhythm for the world. The earth still glowed gold, newly disentangled from the sky and the sea, and no farmer had yet dared to cut into it with a plough.

Gods and goddesses, giants and Titans lived together on the earth, and the fields willingly offered all kinds of fruits and vegetables, though no one had planted them there. In this golden age, no one grew old and frail, but simply passed peacefully on to the Underworld, never looking a day older than twenty-three. Athens did not even exist.

Chaos's children were two shadows called Darkness and Night, and in turn they had a child called Light, who was as different from her parents as anyone could imagine. Meanwhile the earth, who was called Gaia, fell in love with the sky, who was called Ouranos, and they had numerous children. Their first six sons and six daughters were the Titans. They looked just like humans, but each was so big that your eye could not take all of them in at once, no matter how far away you stood. Their next three sons were just as large as the Titans, but had one hundred hands each. The youngest of the children were the Cyclopes, who looked like their brothers and sisters when seen from behind, but had only one eye, planted right in the middle of their foreheads. From these children came all of the gods that the Greeks knew, and later, all of the humans too, though no one yet knew what a human was.

Little Owl couldn't imagine a world before Athens, before gods, humans, farms and wars – before Athena. "So where did the owls live before they came to Athens?" she asked.

Night Owl raised his eyes and gestured to the North, following the coastline with his beak as far as they could make it out. He pointed out across the darkness to Mount Pelion in the distance, where the owls had lived peacefully in one huge family. He explained that the thick forests of pine trees that grew at the very top of this ancient mountain had been his first home. "Would you like to see the old home of the owls?" he asked. And without waiting for a reply, Night Owl bent low to the ancient stone, and raised his wings high above his back. In one whooshing sweep of his wings, he took off. Little Owl took a deep breath and followed.

The owls soared through the night sky in search of their old home. As they flew, Night Owl told Little Owl how there had nearly been no goddess Athena or city of Athens at all.

THE BIRTH OF ZEUS

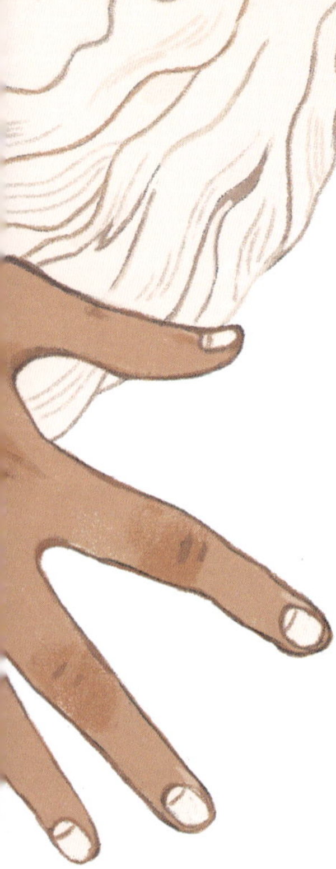

Cronus, the leader of the Titans, lived in fear that his own children would one day grow up and replace him as the ruler of the world. A child of Gaia and Ouranos, Cronus did not know anything of human kindness or family loyalty. In order to prevent his children from usurping his power, Cronus swallowed each and every one of them as soon as they were born. Each time his wife, Rhea, felt an infant kick in her belly, she pleaded with him to forget about his power and let their innocent child live. But no sooner was each infant born than it was snatched immediately from her arms.

Rhea lost five children in this way, but by the time she felt the sixth child growing inside her, she had formed a plan. She escaped to the island of Crete, where she was protected from her husband by the encircling sea. Hidden within a cave, Rhea gave birth to her baby in secret, naming him Zeus. But the sea could not keep Cronus away forever. Only a few days after the birth of Zeus, Rhea began to hear a nervous buzzing among the bee-nymphs who lived nearby. Cronus's ships had arrived. The walls of the cave trembled and echoed with each thud of her husband's giant feet. Rhea had no choice but to leave baby Zeus in the care of the bee-nymphs and face her husband alone. With superhuman strength, she tore one of the rocks from the wall, wrapped it in a soft blanket that she had woven and held it close. Then she kissed Zeus goodbye and stepped out of the cave, leaving her baby son behind.

When Cronus saw his wife cradling what he thought was their newborn son, he could think of nothing but the prophecy he had heard long ago – that one day his own child would kill him and take control of the world. "I've called him Zeus," Rhea said, holding the rock-baby out of her husband's sight so that he would not see through her trick. Cronus snatched the rock-baby from her and, without even opening the folds of the blanket to peek at what lay within, opened his mouth wide like a snake and swallowed it whole. Then, he lifted his wife with one fist and headed back to his ship, covering the whole beach in three of his giant paces. He gave the order to the winds, which carried his ship swiftly away.

Zeus lived with the bee-nymphs in the cave until he was old enough to understand what his father had done to his siblings. He wanted to show his father that what he had done was wrong, so he wandered the island, trying to come up with a plan. One day, while standing at the edge of the shore, he heard a noise between the crashing of the waves that sounded almost like a voice.

Zeus walked on a few paces, until he was up to his ankles in seawater. A young woman rose out of the white foam. He had heard the legend of Metis, a sea nymph who knew how to make magic potions, but he had never seen her for himself. She stretched out her watery hand, and in it Zeus could see a green bottle. He could make out a liquid that fizzed and roiled, even when the bottle was held still.

Zeus couldn't have asked for a more perfect potion. As soon as Cronus drank it, he clutched at his stomach and vomited. Zeus watched his brothers and sisters swim for their lives on the great wave that flowed out of his father's mouth. He counted them as they swam: Hestia, Demeter, Hera, Hades and Poseidon. The last thing to leave Cronus's belly was the rock that he had swallowed instead of his baby son.

Cronus was not happy. He gathered together all of the other Titans from all over the world and declared a war on his children. The war

lasted ten years, but as Zeus and the five other gods and goddesses grew older and stronger, Cronus and the Titans grew weaker and more frail. Just as he began to think the war might go on forever, Zeus had an idea.

The Cyclopes were the best warriors he knew: huge giants who gobbled up great beasts by the fistful. But the Cyclopes could not come. They were imprisoned in an underground dungeon called Tartaros, as far beneath the Underworld as the sky is above the earth. Zeus set off to find them and set them free, for a god does not need a key to open the gates of Tartaros. But just as he was about to enter, Zeus caught sight of a creature he could not have imagined. She was half-woman, half-dragon and around her waist were the heads of fifty wolves, bears, snakes, lions and tigers that snarled and snapped. A long tail with the stinger of a scorpion emerged from her back, and she had a pair of menacing black wings. Kampe walked towards him. As she moved, the snakes around her ankles hissed, and the wolves around her waist howled. But Kampe was no match for the future king of the gods. Zeus struck her down with a power he had not known he possessed: a single flash of lightning. He released the Cyclopes from their cell and led them back up to the top of Mount Olympus. With the Cyclopes on their side, Zeus and his brothers and sisters could not lose.

THE BIRTH OF ATHENA

Zeus was delighted to be reunited with his brothers and sisters, and grateful for Metis's potion. He soon fell in love with the intelligent young woman from the sea, and when she asked him to marry her, he agreed without a moment's hesitation. But it was not long before Zeus too struggled with the same prophecies that had troubled his father. When Metis told him that she was carrying a baby, Zeus could think of nothing but the old prophecy that one day his children would grow up to be more powerful than him. The thought played over and over in Zeus's mind. He snatched up his wife and their unborn child, opened his mouth as wide as he could and swallowed them whole. But Metis was smarter than any king of the gods. She stayed as still as she could, squeezing in between the fleshy parts of Zeus's insides until it was time for her to give birth. While she was waiting, she crafted an intricate suit of armour for her soon-to-be daughter, forging a tiny shield, helmet and spear. Zeus felt the burning of the fire in which Metis shaped the armour, but dismissed it as indigestion.

After some time, Zeus began to suffer from terrible headaches which made him scream so loudly it could be heard across the whole of Mount Olympus. The other gods rushed to see why their king was in such terrible pain. Hephaistos, the god of blacksmiths, was the first to arrive. He had not even had time to put down the great axe that he had been crafting. Hephaistos stared at the king of the gods for a moment. Something seemed to be bulging out of Zeus's head. Bumps shaped like tiny fists sprang up first behind his ear, then above his left eyebrow. Hephaistos lifted his axe and sliced into the top of Zeus's head, making a cut just big enough to free whatever was trapped inside. Zeus gave an almighty scream as he felt the tip of a spear emerge from the wound.

A tiny hand followed, then a tiny helmet and then a tiny shoulder covered with bronze armour, as if ready to go to war. Athena leapt from her father's head and ran off, her bronze shield glinting in the sunshine.

MOUNT PELION

"And did Athena stop the wars when she was born?" Little Owl asked, looking expectantly at her grandfather. Night Owl sighed. "She didn't", he replied eventually. "You see, the humans were struck again and again by the same problem as Zeus and his father. They all wanted to be the most powerful. But the more powerful they became, the less they were able to trust those around them. Athena's birth was the beginning, not the end, of a string of wars that the gods and humans would wage over power until the end of time."

As the two owls flew on, it was so dark they could no longer see their reflections on the surface of the sea. The ground rose sharply upwards, and directly below they saw a mountaintop covered in forest. Or, at least, something that had once been a forest. Now it was little more than a collection of tree stumps, jagged and splintered. "Mount Pelion did not always look like this," Night Owl said as they swooped low over the dry ground. "Once, this place was a forest so full of pines that it became known for its rich greenery. The owls would use it to find their way home on their flights. When those owls from long ago saw the bright, green mountaintop of Mount Pelion, they knew they were home."

NIGHT OWL LOOKED AROUND HIM AND CONTINUED HIS STORY.

THE PUNISHMENT OF PROMETHEUS

Another war broke out, with Zeus's siblings on one side and the Titans on the other. The gods lived on Mount Olympus, a mountain so high that even the Titans, standing on their tiptoes, could not see its peak. Two of the Titans, Otus and Ephialtes, were desperate to look Zeus and his brothers and sisters in the eye. They tore Mount Pelion from the earth and piled it on top of Mount Ossa. Using the mountains like stepping stones, they tried to haul themselves up to the height of Mount Olympus. But Apollo saw them coming, and sent them tumbling down into the Underworld with an almighty kick.

After much bloodshed, the gods emerged victorious. Zeus, in order to punish them, banished all of the Titans to the Underworld. Only Prometheus and his brother Epimetheus were spared, as they had not joined in the war. Zeus gave each of the young men a role in his new world. Epimetheus was commanded to deliver the gifts of the gods to all the living things of Earth. Prometheus was given an even more difficult task: creating humans.

Prometheus got to work immediately. He spent several days carefully shaping a human form out of mud with his fingers. When he had finished, he asked the goddess Athena to breathe life into the figure he had made. Meanwhile, Epimetheus was thoroughly enjoying his task of handing out gifts to all the Earth's creatures. To dogs he gave loyalty, to foxes curiosity, to spiders the ability to weave, and to fish, glimmering scales which helped them slip easily through the sea. Epimetheus was enjoying his job so much that by the time Prometheus's humans had come to life, the bag of gifts was empty. Epimetheus had nothing left to give them.

Prometheus was disappointed in his little brother, but vowed to make it up to the newly-created humans, who were just learning to breathe. He promised them two things. Firstly, that the humans would be the only creatures in the animal kingdom to stand upright on two legs just as the gods did. Secondly, that they would be the only creatures who were able to make fire. But even as he spoke these words, Prometheus knew he was in trouble. Fire, Zeus had told him, belonged to the gods alone. Prometheus pushed that thought to the back of his mind. He stretched up, lit a torch from the flames of the sun and brought it back down to earth. When he saw this flame sinking from the heavens, Zeus was furious. He began concocting the worst punishment he could think of for Prometheus.

Zeus sent Prometheus away to Mount Caucasus, the furthest corner of the world that any god could imagine, and had him chained to an enormous rock. Every day, he sent an eagle to peck and gnaw at Prometheus's liver, tearing out huge chunks of flesh and swallowing them whole. Every night, Zeus repaired Prometheus's liver so that the Titan could not die. Years passed and became centuries, yet still Prometheus could neither move from the rock nor avoid the hungry eagle that came every day to tear at his insides. Every day, Prometheus begged Zeus to release him and send him to the Underworld, but every day Zeus ignored his pleas. He could not die, Zeus said, until someone else agreed to give up their own life for him. Prometheus could not imagine who would ever make such a sacrifice.

PANDORA

Zeus's wrath had not yet been satisfied. He asked Hephaistos, the god of craftsmanship, to create the most beautiful mortal creature imaginable. The gods gave this creature all of the gifts that Epimetheus had given to the animals: intelligence, curiosity, loyalty and many more. They called the creature Pandora. The gods gave her an impossible task. They entrusted her with a jar which she was to keep safe, but was forbidden, under any circumstances, from opening. Then, they sent her down to earth to find Epimetheus.

Although his older brother Prometheus had warned him that Zeus might be plotting further acts of revenge, that thought did not occur to Epimetheus when he saw Pandora on his doorstep. He let her into his home, and the two stayed up all night talking about the mysterious jar. Both of them agreed to respect the gods' wishes, but the gods knew full well that this was impossible. Eventually, overcome by her own curiosity, Pandora slowly twisted the lid...

The jar began to tremble and shake. She stumbled backwards and dropped it to the ground, where it rolled and thrashed violently. With every turn, it released an evil force that Zeus had sealed up inside it. Pandora and Epimetheus watched in horror as envy, pride, hatred, slavery, intolerance, hypocrisy, deceit, unfairness, inequality, mistrust and a thousand other evils flew out on tiny wings. Pandora leapt to her feet and tried to catch them in the folds of her dress, but they were too fast and soon they spread all over the world.

When the jar had finally stopped rolling, Pandora picked it up and looked right down to the bottom. It was not quite empty. One tiny, quivering pair of wings seemed stuck to the bottom of the jar.

These wings were not like the others.

These were golden, and when they flapped they looked like the wings of a swan. She tilted the jar so that she could read the word carved across the middle: έ…λ…π…ί…ς. H O P E.' Pandora turned the jar upside down and shook it. She held it there, waiting to see whether hope would fly away to join the others, but it did not move. She closed the lid and kept hope safe. Without it, humans would have nothing left at all.

CHIRON THE CENTAUR

Chiron lived in a shady cave on Mount Pelion. He was a centaur: a creature with a body that was half-man and half-horse. Chiron was famous for being wise and had been taught all about poetry by the god Apollo. Young people from all over Greece flocked to his cave to listen to him. He was also the son of a Titan, which made him immortal.

Among Chiron's students was a young man named Heracles. Later, the whole world would know of Heracles's strength, but Chiron had known it ever since he had sat cross-legged as a young child at the centaur's feet at only a few years old. Years later, when Heracles had grown up, he returned to Mount Pelion. As soon as he arrived, he went to the house of an old friend of his, and sat down to share a meal with him. To accompany the food, Pholus opened a bottle of wine, not realising that this particular bottle belonged to the god of wine himself, Dionysos. The intoxicating smell of the god's wine wafted through the caves to the other centaurs, who raced through the dark passageways and attacked Pholus, hoping to steal just a single sip.

Heracles reached for his poisoned arrows to fight off the centaurs and, not pausing to aim, he fired in a panic. More and more centaurs rushed in, and Heracles fired arrow after arrow into the crowd in his attempt to defend his friend. Suddenly he heard a shout. "Heracles, it's me, stop!" But it was too late. By the time he had made sense of the words, Heracles had already let go of the bow string. Only when he heard the thud of a centaur's knees dropping to the floor – an arrow fixed firmly in the muscle of his leg – did Heracles recognise the face of his old teacher, Chiron.

Chiron clasped his leg with his hands to try and stop the bleeding, but he could do nothing to stop the pain spreading from the wound. The other centaurs fell silent. The bottle of wine that belonged to Dionysos spilled out onto the floor and was soaked up greedily by the earth, but neither Heracles nor the centaurs noticed. Heracles started to cry. Chiron, being immortal, had never considered his own death before, but at that moment he thought that the pain pulsing through his leg and up into his hip might kill him.

In the days and weeks that followed, Heracles stayed with the wise old centaur, fetching and carrying to reduce the number of times Chiron had to get up from where he was sitting, or walk from one side of the cave to the other. Although he had known Chiron since he was small, Heracles always found that there was more to learn from the centaur, and the two of them never ran out of things to say. One evening, as he sat with Chiron, Heracles told him what had happened to Prometheus and how he had been punished by the gods for bringing fire to the humans.

Chiron was silent. It was difficult for the old teacher, who had dedicated his life to teaching young people to think for themselves, to understand why Zeus had punished the young Titan. Of all the lessons he had taught his students, Chiron valued this one more than any other: "Knowledge for its own sake means nothing at all. Sharing with others is how we grow tall." He had written the words himself on the walls of the cave that was his classroom all those years ago. What crime had Prometheus committed, other than wanting to share the warmth of fire with others? He felt that Prometheus was being unfairly punished.

In his prayers that night, Chiron said this aloud to the gods. He prayed to Zeus that he might be allowed to take Prometheus's place and give up his immortality in exchange. Almost as soon as he had said it, Chiron felt his hooves growing heavy and the sound of metal chains clinking. He felt the surface of a large boulder pressing against his back, and when he blinked and looked around, he found himself on top of an unfamiliar mountain. When he saw a sharp-beaked eagle approaching, heading straight for the fleshy bit below his ribcage, he realised his prayer had come true. Prometheus had been set free, and Chiron would endure forever a punishment that was not meant for him.

However, Chiron did not stay chained to that rock for eternity. Zeus took pity on the centaur who, after all, had not disobeyed him. After three days of agony, Zeus released Chiron from the rock and lifted him up to the skies. He turned every bone in Chiron's body into a little star and bellowed out a promise that was heard by young people all across Greece: whenever they were searching for answers, they had only to look up into the night sky. For as long as there were young people with questions about the world, Chiron would be there, the shape of his body picked out in stars. Zeus named the constellation 'Centaurus', after the half-man, half-horse creatures that made up Chiron's family.

JASON AND THE ARGONAUTS

The first human to cut down a tree with an axe was called Argus. One by one, he chopped down the trees on the top of Mount Pelion, cutting the bark into neat strips and piecing them together like shards of a broken urn until they formed a ship. He called the ship the 'Argo', naming it after himself.

Argus was not alone. It was a man called Jason who had sent him to carry out this task. And it was Jason, not Argus, who needed a ship, to solve a problem that had been created a long time ago.

Jason's uncle Pelias was the son of Tyro, a princess who had fallen in love not with another human as most humans do, but with a river called Enipea. The river, however, did not love her back. Every day, Tyro walked by the river's banks, bending down to stroke the surface of her dark waters with her fingers. Every day she held her breath, plunged her head under the surface of the water and tried to speak to her. But Enipea never answered. Instead, she rushed on downstream away from Tyro, as quickly as she could. One day, something seemed different about the river. When she reached out to touch her surface, Tyro did not feel Enipea rush away from her hand like she usually did. In fact, Tyro was sure that, just for a moment, she had felt the river turn around and flow back towards her. And when she put her head under the water to try to speak to her, a voice answered, "Dive in". The voice was lower than Tyro had imagined it would be, and more commanding, but she ignored her doubts. Tyro tried not to think about the strange, salty taste that lingered on her lips after

she pulled her head back out of the water. She dived in. Only as her hands broke the surface did she realise that this was not running fresh water, but huge salty waves, almost like those of the sea. She froze. The waters that surrounded her were not Enipea's waters at all, but those of the sea god, Poseidon. He had disguised himself as the river Tyro loved so much in order to deceive her. By the time she managed to swim ashore, Tyro was pregnant with twins, Pelias and Neleus.

When the boys grew up, Pelias and Neleus fought violently for the crown of Iolchus, and Pelias – who was older by just a few seconds – won. But he never stopped worrying that one day someone might come along to steal his power. He banished all of Tyro's other sons. He had heard a prophecy that one day, a young man wearing only one sandal would usurp his throne. On good days, he dismissed the idea as ridiculous but on bad days Pelias wandered the streets of Iolchus with his eyes fixed on the floor, counting the sandals of all of the young men who passed him by.

Jason was the son of one of Tyro's exiled sons, and even before he was born it was clear that Pelias was not going to cope well with this threat to his power. He stayed clear of the house in which Jason's mother lived, and even the sight of baby-sized sandals in the marketplace made him feel nervous. Jason's mother devised a plan to keep her son safe from the king.

As soon as Jason was born, she commanded all of the women in the palace to wail and cry so that Pelias would think that the baby had not survived. A funeral was planned, and while it was taking place, Jason's mother slipped him out of the back door and up to the caves on Mount Pelion. She gave him to the centaur Chiron to raise as his own, knowing that her son would be safe on the mountain. After many years, Jason left

Pelion – a place he had come to call home – in search of Iolchus, the town he was born in. As he was travelling, he passed an elderly woman who was standing ankle-deep in a river, struggling to cross it. Jason stopped and offered her his arm to guide her across.

As she reached the shore, the old woman began to transform, and before Jason knew what was happening, he found himself standing in front of the goddess Hera. Jason recognised her as the goddess of marriage and families, and considered this to be a good omen. Hera promised that she would protect him, and she never forgot her promise. He was so overcome by amazement that it wasn't until he had walked all the way up the grassy riverbank and onto the jagged, rocky ground that he noticed that he had lost one of his sandals. He thought nothing of it, except that it was quite uncomfortable to cross the stony ground with a sandal missing. And so, he carried on towards Iolchus.

As soon as Jason arrived, Pelias looked down and saw his feet, remembering the prophet's words. "What would you do," Pelias asked Jason, "if you had been told by a prophet that you would

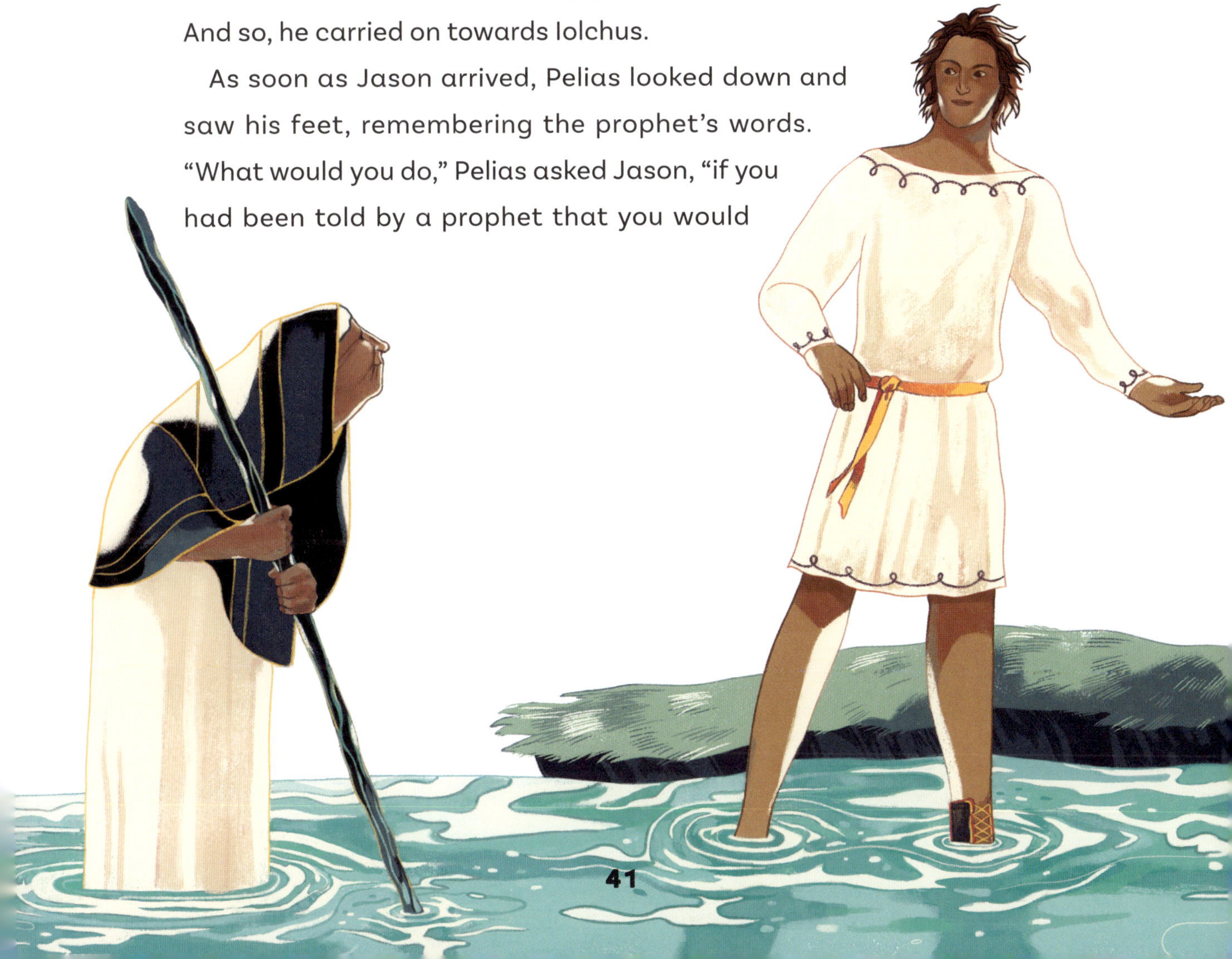

be killed by a young man wearing only one sandal, and then you crossed paths with a young man whom you had never met, but who was wearing only one sandal?" Jason couldn't help but laugh, though he tried to hide his amusement from the paranoid king. He answered immediately, "I would give him an impossible task," he said, "something at which I knew he would never succeed." Jason was surprised by his own brave words, until he realised that it was the goddess Hera who had given him this courage.

"Fetch me..." Pelias thought for a moment. "The golden fleece," he said. Jason had never heard of the golden fleece before. He asked the king to tell him more. Pelias told him the legend of a flying sheep with golden curls. Its fleece had been given as a gift to King Aeetes, and hung in a grove in Colchis, a faraway kingdom. It was guarded by a huge dragon that never slept. Both Jason and his uncle Pelias were sure that to fetch the golden fleece and bring it back to Iolchus was indeed an impossible feat.

But Hera knew differently. She advised Jason to assemble the strongest people he knew for a crew she nicknamed the 'Argonauts', and to hollow out the trunk of a tree. This was to become a ship, though humans did not yet know what a ship was. Jason called Argus and asked him to build a seafaring vessel from the strongest pines that grew on Mount Pelion. When the ship was ready, they set out.

First, the crew came to the island of Lemnos, a place where women lived without any men, and were ruled by Queen Hypsipyle. Some of the men in the crew felt uncomfortable. Life here was very different to what they were used to in Iolchus. There was no place for men on Lemnos so they returned to their ship and continued on their travels. Next, they came to the island of the Doliones people, where they were greeted with warm hospitality by the

friendly king, Cyzicus. King Cyzicus was an optimistic ruler, and he did not want to trouble the sailors with stories of the dangerous creatures that inhabited his kingdom. Besides, he thought, as long as they never ventured into the dark forest at the island's edge, the Argonauts would never have to worry about the monsters that lived within it.

Jason and his men went to gather food for the rest of their journey, leaving Heracles, the strongest of the Argonauts, to guard the ship. Heracles was sure that he must have dozed off, because a short time later he saw a crowd of six-armed giants emerging from the forest – this had to be a dream! The giants, who were much more real than he would have liked them to be, surged forwards. But even these creatures with their colossal limbs were no match for Heracles. He only needed to defeat a few of them before the rest fled back into the forest in fear.

When the Argonauts returned, it wasn't long before Heracles realised that six-armed giants were the least of his problems. As he counted his friends boarding the ship, he noticed that someone was missing: Hylas. Heracles had entrusted Hylas with all of his secrets, and he loved him in a way that was different to his love for all of the other Argonauts, though Heracles had never had the courage to tell him. He called for Jason and demanded to know what had happened to Hylas, though he knew, even before his leader began to speak, that he would never see him again. Heracles was inconsolable when Jason told him what had happened.

As the Argonauts were returning from the forest, Hylas had stopped to admire a pine tree that reminded him of the ones he had known on Mount Pelion. While he stood there, he heard something that sounded at first like whispering, then like singing, coming from a puddle of water nearby.

He knelt down so that he could hear better. He had never heard nymphs sing before, though he had heard legends of their enchanting voices. The nymphs fell in love with Hylas instantly – which did not surprise Heracles one bit when he later heard the story – and they reached out to take hold of him with their muddy, icy hands. They pulled him into the water, not realising that Hylas was a human who could not survive with them beneath the surface. Hylas was lost to the watery depths. Heracles was devastated by the loss of the man he loved. He crumpled into the sand and cried for a whole day and a whole night before his friends picked him up and carried him aboard so that they could set sail again.

The Argo sailed on for just a short while before reaching the court of King Phineus, a man who had been starved for so long that he almost

disappeared when he turned sideways. Phineus was also blind, and those who disliked him said that this was his punishment from the gods for revealing the future to someone who should not have known it. But in fact the gods had punished Phineus in another way: they had sent the harpies to torture him. They were huge, powerful birds with women's faces and savage talons that could rip off a man's head in a single swipe. The Argonauts watched as the harpies swooped down and devoured all of the food on Phineus's table before he could take a single mouthful. Jason and his friends could not stand by and watch the man go hungry any longer. They chased the harpies to the steep cliffs at the edge of the island. The beasts scrambled to avoid tumbling into the sea. As the bird-women clutched the cliffside with their talons, a rainbow darted across the sky above the ocean. The brightly-coloured goddess Iris, the kinder sister of the cruel harpies, appeared. She begged the Argonauts not to chase her sisters into the sea, and promised that the harpies would never bother Phineus and his people again. The Argonauts agreed, and Phineus tucked into his first meal in decades. He would never forget what a blessing it was to have a full belly, and he promised to help the Argonauts in any way he could.

King Phineus told Jason that the only way to get to Colchis and find the golden fleece was to go through the clashing rocks. He begged the Argonauts to proceed with great caution, for these two towering rocks were famous for smashing themselves together whenever a ship tried to pass between them, crushing everything in their path. But Phineus had a plan to avoid sharing the fate of thousands of ships before them. “Release a white dove,” he advised, “to fly ahead of your ship between the rocks. Then, row as fast as you can, and don’t stop until you are well clear of danger.” The advice to row fast towards the rocks sounded a bit strange to the Argonauts, but Jason was not in a position to argue. He thanked Phineus, and vowed to do as he had been instructed. As they approached the rocks, Jason opened a small cage and let out a single white dove. The clashing rocks rushed together, but the dove flew swiftly between them, losing only a couple of tail feathers as it made its escape. As the giant cliffs crunched together, Jason ordered the Argonauts to row with all their might. As they approached, the rocks were beginning to separate. Because they were too heavy to change direction and move towards each other again quickly enough, the Argo slipped through. The rocks ground to a halt, as if unsure what to do. Now that they were out of sync, the clashing rocks froze in place and were never able to smash passing ships again.

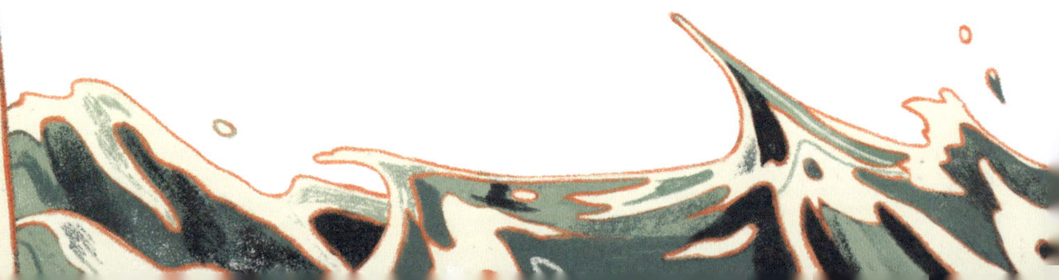

JASON MEETS MEDEA

Eventually the Argo arrived in Colchis, where King Aeetes kept the golden fleece. Jason thought long and hard about how to defeat the dragon that never slept. Meanwhile, the goddess Hera had already hatched a secret plan. She had been watching Jason closely and decided it was time to reward the young man who had helped her cross the river all those years ago. So she went to visit Aphrodite, the goddess of love and beauty, to ask for help. It was simple enough for Aphrodite to click her fingers and make the king's daughter, Medea, fall instantly in love. Hera knew that with Medea's help, Jason had a chance of completing his impossible task.

It was not long before Jason came to love Medea in return. The two were inseparable, and Jason would spend whole days and nights listening to Medea talk about the different magical powers of all of the plants that grew in Colchis. He loved how much she knew, the way she talked about the potions and remedies she concocted, and that she seemed to be able to create a magical elixir from whatever she found. Slowly, it dawned on him that her knowledge might be exactly what he needed to trick the dragon and snatch the golden fleece.

As soon as he explained, Medea understood exactly what she needed to do. She plucked leaves and petals from plants Jason had never seen before, speaking their names under her breath. When she had finished mixing them

together, she pressed a stone jar into Jason's hand, kissed him and led him to the grove where her father King Aeetes kept the golden fleece. A shiver ran down Jason's spine when he saw the ever-watchful dragon fix its eyes on him. He slowly turned the lid of the small stone jar until it popped open, and a dark liquid oozed out onto the ground towards the dragon. It smelt like poppy seeds and the dried bark of an ebony tree. The dragon's head grew heavy and its eyes drooped, until it finally fell to the ground with a dull thud that made the grass tremble and the trees shake. It had fallen asleep. Jason tiptoed past the beast, reached up and pulled the golden fleece down from the tree where it was hanging. As he ran his fingers through the golden curls, he could not believe what, between the two of them, they had managed to do.

Jason rushed to the edge of the water, where Medea had prepared their ships to escape. Clutching the golden fleece in one hand and Medea's hand tightly in the other, he helped her to lift her younger brother Absyrtus onto the deck of the Argo. Jason called out to his friends to row as fast as they could, and the ship began to pick up speed. But just when he thought they had put a safe distance between themselves and Colchis, he turned around to find that a ship even larger than their own was behind them and gaining speed, for it had twice as many rowers. At its helm was a man Medea recognised immediately: her father.

Though Jason called to the Argonauts to row even faster, they were already pushing and straining as hard as they could. The ships were now close enough that Jason could have crossed the gap between them with a single leap. He looked to Medea, whose eyes were fixed on her brother Absyrtus. She realised that it must have been him who had tipped their father off about their escape. With the sudden rage that comes from the sharp sting of betrayal, Medea made a decision she would regret forever. She took hold of her brother's shoulders, and with her own two hands she tore Absyrtus into pieces. She held the pieces of her brother over the side of the ship with her arms outstretched, sprinkling them into the water below. King Aeetes screamed with agony as, piece by piece, his son's body fell into the waves below, and he begged his rowers to stop. He refused to go any further until he had collected every last bit of of Absyrtus and placed the pieces together like a puzzle on the sand. By the time he had finished, Jason, Medea and the Argo had vanished from sight.

MOUNT PARNASSUS

Little Owl scratched the ground impatiently. "What happened then? Was that the end of the story?"

Night Owl laughed. "Well, maybe for Absyrtus," he said, "but not for Jason." He told her that although Jason did eventually make it back to Iolchus with Medea and the golden fleece, their happiness did not last for long.

It was the end of this story, however, for the owls who lived in the forests of Mount Pelion. Night Owl explained that after the first pine tree had been cut down from the top of Mount Pelion to build the Argo, the golden age was over. The owls couldn't remain on Mount Pelion. The ground was too hot now that there were no trees to block out the sun, and they could not stand to watch as their homes came crashing to the ground. They headed south in search of cooler nights, fatter mice and, most importantly, fewer humans. With that tale told, Night Owl took off again, with Little Owl at his heels.

The two owls eventually came to another mountain, whose peak was shaded by trees. Night Owl called it Mount Parnassus, and he explained to Little Owl that this had been the place the owls had fled to after the trees on Mount Pelion had been cut down.

"Parna," Night Owl said, meant "home," in a language so old that no one speaks it anymore.

"And was it?" Little Owl asked, as they landed on a branch. "Your home, I mean?"

"It was a home," Night Owl replied, "but not for forever."

As she listened to Night Owl, Little Owl became aware of a strange humming sound. Then another voice joined in the humming. Then another. "Can you hear that?" Little Owl asked.

"Hear what?" said Night Owl, but Little Owl could tell by the way the feathers turned up mischievously around his beak that he knew what she meant. "Oh, that's just the trees singing," he said.

"Trees can't sing!" Little Owl giggled.

"They can here," Night Owl said. "Listen."

Sure enough, as she listened, Little Owl could make out the voices of the trees that surrounded her. Night Owl explained that this mountain belonged to Apollo, the god of poetry and music, who was also responsible for the rising and setting of the sun.

"Parnassus," Night Owl said, "was where owls learnt to keep their promises." He settled down on his branch to tell Little Owl the story of Orpheus, the singer who lived on Mount Parnassus. The music of Orpheus was legendary, but his talent could not save him when he failed to keep his promise.

Night Owl took a deep breath and was just about to begin, when a huge gust of wind threw the two owls from their perch. Little Owl and Night Owl spread their wings and landed gently on the ground at the foot of the tree. They looked up and saw a huge white stallion, his mane glittering with stars, soaring above them, whinnying at something they could not see. The beating of his golden wings had blown all the needles from the fir tree onto the ground.

"Welcome to Parnassus," a loud voice boomed from the sky. "I am Pegasus." Little Owl was shocked.

Here on Mount Parnassus, birds were not the only ones who could fly! With a toss of his incredible mane, Pegasus took off into the night sky, far faster than even an owl could follow.

"Now you've met Pegasus!" chuckled Night Owl.

PEGASUS AND BELLEROPHON

Pegasus was famous all over Greece for his friendship with the great hero, Bellerophon. Together they had defeated the Chimera, a fierce monster with the heads of a lion and a goat, and a snake for a tail. Although the gods were delighted that the Chimera was dead, Bellerophon was not satisfied. He'd had a taste of glory, and he wanted more and more of it. One day he decided to ride Pegasus higher than ever before, high enough to reach Mount Olympus, the highest point of the known world, where the gods lived.

Bellerophon knew that humans were not allowed to cross the boundary that separated them from the gods, but he was too full of pride to take any notice of the rules. As soon as Zeus saw a bright white horse with golden wings galloping through the sky towards him, he knew its rider must be Bellerophon. The king of the gods decided to show the hero just how easily distracted his noble steed could be. He plucked a tiny gadfly from the air and sent it buzzing towards Pegasus who, for a moment, forgot that he was a magical flying stallion at all, and bucked and kicked at the fly like any old donkey would. Bellerophon lost his grip on Pegasus and fell to earth, where he wandered for the rest of time, alone.

THE DISCOVERY OF LYKOREIA

Before he met Bellerophon, Pegasus had always lived on the marble cliffs on the north side of Mount Parnassus. But the people of Lykoreia, whose home was also on this side of the mountain, had not always lived so high up. Long ago, they lived in the shady forest at the bottom, their little town hidden from sight by trees and divided down the middle by a river. The river was their lifeblood. They drank from it, bathed in it and played in it every day. Some say that they took the river for granted.

One day the river turned against them. Whether it had been driven by a god or angered by a mortal they couldn't tell, but the water began to rise and kept on coming. It rushed through their homes and put out the cooking fires. Families took whatever they could carry, and fled. They tried to walk up the mountain paths, hoping that if they could get close enough to the sun its warmth would dry them. Their efforts were hopeless. The marble cliffs became slippery under their feet and they could not see the path they were following through the dark water. The older and weaker members at the back could not keep up.

Just as they were about to give up and let the waters wash them back down to the forest, a girl named Kora stopped so suddenly that those behind tripped over her. "Can't you hear that?" she whispered. The Lykoreians shook their heads, thinking the little girl must have imagined a noise. The cry came again, louder this time, sounding almost mournful. Kora was sure that she could make out specks of white moving quickly over the stones across the valley. It was a pack of wolves, calling to each other, leading the way to somewhere safer. Kora took off at a run with the Lykoreians following at her heels. They had to tread carefully to avoid slipping off the cliff edge. But the deep pawprints of the wolves provided the perfect footholds, and the Lykoreians kept inching forwards.

After what seemed like a lifetime, the families arrived at the very top of Mount Parnassus and felt dry stone under their feet. They set about rebuilding their homes. Every morning, Kora would climb onto the roof of her family's small house, searching for the wolves in the distance. She never saw them again, but Kora knew what she had seen that day had been real. They called their town 'Lykoreia', a name that meant 'the howling of the wolves', after the sound that had led them to their new home.

ORPHEUS AND EURYDICE

It was also here, on Mount Parnassus, that the Muses lived. These nine sisters had voices more beautiful than any mortal could imagine, and they could write stories and songs long before most poets or singers had even thought of them.

The eldest of the sisters, Calliope, had a young son called Orpheus. One day, when Orpheus was playing in the dust, he felt a chill on the back of his neck and looked around to see the god Apollo casting a shadow over him. Apollo said nothing, but took something from the folds of his toga and placed it on the ground between them. Orpheus had never seen anything like it before. It looked like the shell of a tortoise, but had two long horns pointing out of the top. The horns sloped away from each other, and between them were strung seven taut hairs from the mane of a white horse. Just as Orpheus was about to reach for the curious object, Apollo spoke in a voice so deep and melodic that Orpheus could not tell

whether he was speaking or singing. "Have you never seen a lyre before, Orpheus?" Orpheus had not, but he took the lyre and rested it on his knee so that he could get a closer look. He plucked at one of the horse hairs. A single musical note rang out. He jumped back, dropping the tortoise shell on the ground. "You'll learn," Apollo said, half-speaking and half-singing again. By the time Orpheus had brushed the dust from the lyre and placed it back on his knee, the god had disappeared.

Orpheus did learn. He practised sad songs with his mother, happy songs with his aunt Thalia, and love songs with his aunt Erato. He practised until he could play a tune for every kind of dance his aunt Terpsichore knew, and until he knew the perfect note for every star that his aunt Urania could think of. His music became well known all over Greece, and not just among humans. When Orpheus played in the forest, even the trees seemed to sway in time to the music. He never forgot the gift Apollo had given him, and the two remained friends. When he was old enough, Orpheus married one of Apollo's daughters, Eurydice. She was tall, as strong as an oak tree, and always had plenty to say. Everyone agreed that they were perfect for each other. But when Hymen, the god of marriage, heard the songs that Orpheus sang at their wedding and saw the couple dancing in the meadow, he blinked back a tear. "This will not last," was all that he would say.

Later that night, when Eurydice was walking back from the meadow, she saw the shepherd Aristaeus in the distance. She recognised him immediately, because she had known him since she was a child. But tonight there was a strange coldness in his eyes. Instead of raising his hand in a friendly wave, he suddenly ran towards her. Eurydice turned and fled, not looking where she placed her feet. She had only made it halfway back to the meadow when she felt two sharp fangs pierce her left ankle. The pain darted through her leg and into her stomach, rising through her chest until she was unable to breathe. Eurydice dropped to the ground. Her soul slipped from her body and began its slow descent into the Underworld. The venomous snake that had bitten her slithered over her foot and into the bushes nearby.

When Orpheus discovered what had happened to his wife, he was inconsolable. He picked up his lyre and played the saddest songs he knew, all day and all night, stopping only to wipe the tears from his eyes. As he played, the nymphs that lived in the streams began to cry. The trees wept and the rocks tried to hide their tears. The sweet, sad melody spread far and wide, and soon Orpheus felt a familiar cold shadow on the back of his neck. The low, melodic voice of Apollo echoed across the mountain: "Go to the gates of Sparta as quickly as you can. Ask for Charon, the ferryman, and tell him that you need to cross the river Styx." Orpheus began to play more quickly, and all of Greece could hear that he was afraid. Humans, he knew, could not cross the river Styx and return alive. As if he had heard his thoughts, Apollo continued, "That's the easy bit. Once you have crossed the river, you must get past a huge dog with three heads. Only then will you be able to ask Hades and Persephone to let you take Eurydice back to the land of the living." Orpheus opened his mouth to answer, but as he did so he felt the warmth of the sun wash over him again. Apollo had gone.

Orpheus picked up his lyre and ran to the gates of Sparta as fast as he could. When he arrived at the banks of the river Styx, he was out of breath, and Charon the ferryman approached him before he had chance to speak. The old man held a long stick in his hand that he used to push the boat along the Styx. His eyes lit up with blue flames while he spoke. "Jump in, dead man." His voice sounded like iron scraping on stone. Orpheus opened his mouth to explain that he had not died, but he could

not think of the words. He reached for his lyre, as music was the only way he knew how to speak, and played the song he had played on the day of Eurydice's death. The ferryman's flashing eyes dimmed to flickers, and a single tear fell into his lap.

Charon started to row, and each stroke pushed them further into darkness. Suddenly the boat juddered to a halt. Orpheus climbed onto the bank on the other side of the river and watched as the old ferryman rowed back towards the sunlight. The ground moved beneath his feet, rising and falling in a steady rhythm. He realised he wasn't standing on the riverbank at all, but on some kind of huge beast. Orpheus squinted in the darkness. He was standing on the most enormous dog he had ever seen, and it had – he counted – three heads! All six of its eyes were closed, but Orpheus could make out three sets of sharp teeth. He tiptoed across its ribcage and jumped off its shoulders, plucking slow, sleepy notes on the lyre and singing a hypnotic tune. The beast did not wake.

He crept onwards, deeper into the Underworld, and soon heard a woman crying somewhere in the distance. Her sobs echoed through the darkness and he followed the sound until he was close enough to make out what she was saying. "What is that sad music?" By now, Orpheus was close enough that he could see the shadowy form of Persephone, who was sitting limply in her chair as Hades tried in vain to comfort her. "My wife..." Orpheus began "...she was bitten by a snake, and now she's here. I came to get her back." He plucked the sad song on his lyre one last time. Both Hades and Persephone were overwhelmed with his sorrow and agreed to let Orpheus lead his wife back to the land of the living. But they had one condition.

"Until you have passed through the gates to the Underworld and can feel the sun on your face, you must not look back. Do you give me your word?" said Persephone, fixing him with an icy stare. "I promise," Orpheus replied.

Trusting that his wife was following behind him, he stepped back into the ferry boat to cross the Styx, careful not to look behind him even as he turned to sit down. When he reached the other side, he began the long uphill walk towards the land of the living.

Orpheus walked slowly, planting his feet heavily in the dust to make sure that his wife could trace each footprint. A stream of light shone in through the gates up ahead, where he could see a queue of souls waiting for their ferry to the Underworld. Orpheus kept his eyes fixed firmly on the ground in front of him and carried on.

Gradually the wet rocks fell away and the darkness began to lift. The land of the living was mere steps away when Orpheus started to panic. He could no longer hear Eurydice's footsteps keeping rhythm behind him.

He remembered Persephone's words: "You must not look back." They played over and over in his head until they took on a melody of their own. Orpheus took another step. The tune continued playing, and soon he forgot that there had ever been words at all. Slowly, he turned his head, desperate to catch sight of Eurydice. For a moment, he saw her and she raised her eyes to meet his.

He reached out to wrap his arms around Eurydice, but she instantly vanished, leaving him clutching at thin air. Orpheus had broken his promise.

THE CITY OF THEBES

"Did he ever see her again?" Little Owl asked.

"He did. But not alive," Night Owl replied. "Orpheus never gave up his search for Eurydice. He returned to the Underworld again and again until eventually he prayed for his own death to come so that he could see his wife. The gods granted his wish and the two were reunited at last, laughing and making music in the Elysian fields for all time."

"Now that you have seen where the owls came from," said Night Owl, "it's time to fly home."

Night Owl and Little Owl flew south-east until the ground beneath them took on a strange, dark-red colour. When they swooped down to investigate, they saw that beneath them was a muddy field studded with hundreds of gaping holes, each of them big enough to hold a human.

Crows were circling the field, digging amongst the holes for scraps to eat. First one arrived, then two, and soon there were so many that they formed an intimidating crowd. Little Owl stuck close to her grandfather and kept out of their way. She could hear the crows bickering and whispering about them as they picked at the bones.

Ahead of them were seven huge stone gates. Little Owl was frightened. The city they were in was nothing like Athens. This place didn't feel like it could be a home to anyone.

"Why are there holes in the ground?" she asked. "...And so many bones?"

"Long before the owls arrived," said Night Owl, "the city of Thebes had been nothing but a cold-water spring with a single yellow flower growing beside it. Cadmus, the first king of Thebes, discovered it almost by accident. When he was a young man, the Oracle at Delphi commanded him to follow a cow that had a strange moon-shaped mark on her back. Wherever the cow first stopped, the Oracle said, would be the site of the city that he would rule.

Cadmus liked the idea of being a king, so he followed closely in the tracks of the cow for several days without stopping. She led him east until eventually they came to a field that was thick with grass, with a clear, cold stream and a single yellow flower. As he approached the spring, Cadmus heard a sound that he thought was a bit like a crow, only a hundred times louder and more frightening.

The grass around him began to shiver, and suddenly an enormous dragon slithered out of the spring, straight towards Cadmus. With barely a moment to react, he reached for his sword and slayed the dragon in one stroke."

Little Owl knew what happened next. "Is that when Athena appeared?" she said, excitedly.

"It is," replied Night Owl. "And she told Cadmus to pluck out the dragon's teeth, one by one, and plant them in the ground like seeds. Cadmus did as he was told. As he turned to leave, a great cloud of soil billowed up behind him. From each spot where he had buried a dragon's tooth, a man in a full set of battle armour sprang up. Cadmus was stunned. Fearing that they would attack him, he picked up the largest rock he could find and threw it into the field amongst the newly-sprouted men. The men, not knowing who had thrown the rock, immediately blamed one another. They took up arms and each killed as many of their brothers as they could manage. Only five survived, and those men became the first Thebans."

"They killed their own brothers?" Little Owl was shocked.

"It was not easy to be a family in Thebes," Night Owl said ominously. "Thebes was a dark, shady kind of place, where it was difficult to see things clearly and people were not always who they seemed to be."

OEDIPUS AND JOCASTA

Laius and Jocasta were King and Queen of Thebes many generations after Cadmus and the men born from dragon's teeth. Shortly after the birth of their son Oedipus, they heard a terrible prophecy from the Oracle at Delphi. The Oracle was a woman who the god Apollo had made able to see the future, and her prophecy for Laius and Jocasta was perhaps the worst one she had ever had to tell. She told the king and queen that their child would one day kill his father and marry his own mother. In a desperate attempt to avoid the prophecy, they decided to put as much distance as possible between themselves and their son. Laius, with tears of remorse in his eyes, pierced holes in his child's ankles so that he could not crawl away, and ordered a shepherd to leave their infant son on the side of the mountain to die. But the shepherd could not do it. When he looked at the baby, he thought of his own infant son who was safe at home. Instead of obeying the king's orders, he gave the baby to another shepherd, Polybus, who lived higher up the mountain. Polybus and his wife Merope had not been able to have children of their own. They raised Oedipus as their own son, with all the love and laughter that any child could hope for.

Years later, Oedipus met a mysterious man who insisted that he knew a secret about him. He told Oedipus that Polybus was not his real father. Oedipus could not believe it. He went straight to Delphi to consult the Oracle and find out the truth. The Oracle repeated the same words she had spoken nearly two decades earlier to King Laius and Queen Jocasta: that Oedipus was destined to kill his father and marry his mother. Struck with fear that he might hurt Polybus and Merope, Oedipus fled, never to return.

Eventually he came to a crossroads where three roads met. Oedipus approached with great caution, for he knew that many travellers who had come to these crossroads had never returned. Out of the corner of his eye he saw a band of men heading towards him. They moved quickly, and Oedipus thought he could see the glint of swords in the sunlight. Thinking that he was about to be attacked, he drew his sword and killed all but one of them, who fled too fast for Oedipus to follow.

Oedipus continued along the road, relieved to have escaped. Eventually he came to the gates of Thebes. There, he was stopped by a sphinx, a large monster with the head of a woman, the body of a lion and wings so enormous that they blocked the light. The Sphinx looked down at him from the top of the gate and spoke in her mysterious voice. "No one goes into Thebes without answering my riddle," she said. Oedipus's stomach lurched as he noticed, lying between the Sphinx's paws, the chewed-up bones of those who had answered the riddle incorrectly. "Proceed," Oedipus squeaked, and he listened intently to the riddle. "Which creature walks on four legs

in the morning, two legs in the afternoon and three legs in the evening?" The Sphinx gave a deep belly laugh. It was clear that many had answered the riddle incorrectly before. Oedipus paused, racking his brains for an answer. He thought of his father Polybus, who he loved so much that he had left home to keep him safe. Polybus was now growing old and used a stick to help him walk. From a distance, the stick almost looked like a third leg! Oedipus stammered, "M-m-man. Man. Humans, I mean. Because a baby crawls on all fours, an adult walks on two legs and the elderly use sticks to walk as if they had three legs." The Sphinx was stunned to hear the correct answer to her riddle. Silent in shock, she fell from her perch, and crashed, dead, into the dust below.

Oedipus continued into Thebes, where he found a city mourning the loss of King Laius. The Thebans were told he had been killed by a band of highway robbers. Upon learning that Oedipus had solved the riddle of the Sphinx, the people of Thebes immediately named him their new king. He moved into the palace and married the queen, Jocasta. Oedipus and Jocasta got along so well, they could hardly believe that they had never met before. They had two sons, Polyneices and Eteocles, and two daughters, Antigone and Ismene.

Many years later, Thebes began to suffer from a terrible plague. The Thebans tried everything – they prayed to the gods, burned incense and made sacrifices. But their efforts were in vain. Everyone who lived in Thebes lost a neighbour, a parent, a brother, a sister or a child to the plague. King Oedipus stood in front of his grieving people and promised that he would find a cure. The citizens believed him. This was, after all, the man who had already done an impossible thing, and answered the riddle of the Sphinx. Oedipus went once again to Delphi to consult the Oracle, who told him that the murderer of King Laius was now living in the city of

Thebes. She added that the only way to get rid of the plague was to send whoever had killed Laius into exile. Oedipus heard her words and promised to do so. When he returned to Thebes, he swore in front of all of the citizens that he would find the person who had killed King Laius and punish them with exile. The crows circling above him laughed, for they knew that the murderer Oedipus was searching for was none other than himself.

Oedipus sent for Tiresias, the same prophet who had been advising kings of Thebes since the days of Cadmus. Tiresias was blind, but he could see more than most people could, because the gods had made him a prophet. When he asked Tiresias to tell him who had killed Laius, the old man simply shook his head and said, "A king should not ask questions that he does not want the answer to." He pleaded with Oedipus to let him go, knowing what the truth would do to his king. It was not until Oedipus threatened to lay

the blame on Tiresias himself that the prophet told him the truth. “You”, he said. “You are the cause of the plague. You killed your own father and the king of Thebes in one stroke.” Oedipus did not believe it and made fun of him, saying that his blindness had spread from his eyes to his mind (even though he knew full well that blindness did not work that way). “You may have sight,” Tiresias answered, shaking his head, “but you cannot truly see.” He gestured toward Oedipus’s ankles, at the swollen holes pierced by his father Laius, which had never properly healed. “Your father Laius abandoned you, when you were just a baby.” Tiresias told Oedipus about the prophecy that said Laius would be killed by his own son. Oedipus tried not to listen but he began to understand. He banished Tiresias from his sight, vowing never to listen to his prophecies again.

Oedipus sent a messenger to find the man who had fled from him during the fight at the crossroads long ago. This man was there, Oedipus thought, so he will be able to tell everyone that it was not King Laius who was killed on that day. The man was eventually found in the fields not far from Thebes, where he was working as a shepherd. Oedipus quizzed him angrily, wanting to know who he had been travelling with on that day many years ago. The shepherd held his breath. He knew who Oedipus was and could think of no way out. He told his king the truth: it was Laius he had been travelling with that day. Oedipus was both Laius’s son and his murderer.

Oedipus, horrified, rushed home to find Jocasta. But when he opened the bedroom door, he found her dead. He had arrived too late. Oedipus saw all too clearly what had happened, and he could no longer bear to see at all. He took the golden pins from Jocasta's dress and pressed them into his eyes. Then he fled from Thebes, leaving his royal palace and family behind. Only his daughter Antigone went with him.

ANTIGONE

The troubles for Oedipus's family did not end with him. After their father went into exile from his own city, Oedipus's two sons Polyneices and Eteocles were given the task of ruling Thebes. Since they could not agree on who would be king, the brothers decided that they would share the throne. Eteocles would rule for one year, and then as soon as the birds flew south for the winter, Polyneices would take over for the next year.

The arrangement worked well at first, but when the nights started to grow colder and the birds started to leave their nests to seek warmer lands, Eteocles refused to leave the throne. Enraged with his brother for breaking his word, Polyneices went to Athens and then to Argos to seek help in overthrowing Eteocles. He secured the alliance of King Theseus and King Adrastus. But King Adrastus of Argos also shared his throne – not with his brother, but with the prophet Amphiarus, who could see the future. When Polyneices asked Amphiarus to take part in the war to win Thebes back from Eteocles, he immediately refused. He knew that this war would be the cause of his death. "The problem with being a prophet," he said, "is that death never comes as a surprise."

But Polyneices knew that Amphiarus had a weakness. He loved his wife Eriphyle so much that he would not refuse anything she asked. Polyneices had to get Eriphyle on his side. He eventually persuaded her to discuss the matter with Amphiarus, and it was not long before Polyneices and his horses were on the road to Thebes with King Theseus, King Adrastus and the prophet (who would not stop talking about the doom that was about to befall them). Their armies fought each other for weeks before finally, the day came when Eteocles and Polyneices met on the battlefield. The brothers struck each other down at the same moment, and both died that day.

Soon after the deaths of the two brothers, their Uncle Creon took over as king of Thebes. Creon had fought on Eteocles's side, and declared that Polyneices was a traitor to the city. As a traitor, his body could not be buried, and was to be left out on the field to be eaten by crows. Creon passed a law: anyone who buried Polyneices would be put to death. None of the Thebans were brave enough to disagree except Antigone.

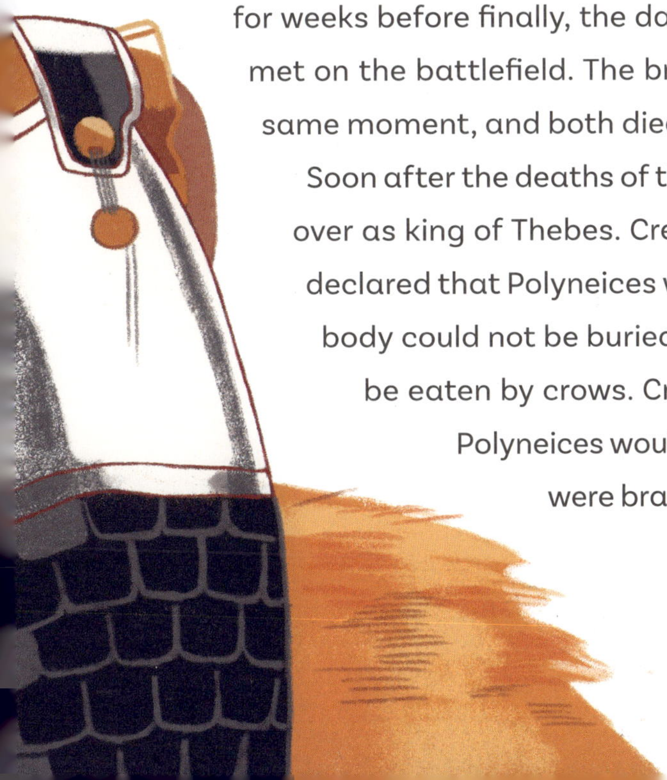

She could not bear to see her beloved brother denied a proper burial, or to think of his soul floating around the Earth for eternity. She broke Creon's law. Just as she was sprinkling a last handful of dust on top of her brother's body, Creon's soldiers appeared. Antigone did not even try to deny that she had buried him. In fact, she was glad that she had defied the king, because she believed she had done the right thing. Creon remained true to his word, imprisoning Antigone in a cave underground where she was left to die.

Many tried to change Creon's mind - even his own son Haemon, who was in love with Antigone. Haemon told his father that he did not know what he would do without Antigone, who he loved so much. But Creon could not be convinced. Eventually, the prophet Tiresias, who had always spoken honestly to the kings of Thebes, told Creon that he was being cruel and unjust. Creon sent his soldiers to the cave to release Antigone, but having been trapped in the cave for days on end with no food or water, she had died before the soldiers reached her. The news that he had lost the woman he loved made Haemon's heart stop. Later that night Haemon's mother died too, from grief at the loss of her son. Creon lost his niece, his wife and his son in a single night.

ECHO AND NARCISSUS

It was not just the kings who received wisdom from the prophet Tiresias. Narcissus's mother remembered well the prophecy that Tiresias had made to her when her son was born: "Your son will live a long life, as long as he does not seek to know himself." Terrified of what the prophecy hinted, she ordered all mirrors and shiny surfaces to be removed from her home. Narcissus would never know what he looked like.

It was no wonder that her son sought out his own reflection, though, because everyone else could not stop looking at him. All the nymphs in the forests that bordered the city of Thebes were in love with Narcissus. Ever since he was a boy, people would stop to take a look at him. None of them could quite say why – none of them, that is, except Echo, the nymph who could not help but speak her mind. And although no one who knew her could imagine her lost for words, when she finally met Narcissus, Echo was speechless.

The goddess Hera had done this to her. Hera had failed in her attempts to catch her husband Zeus flirting with the forest nymphs, because each time she neared the grove where they lived, Echo would greet her and launch into a story of some distant land where horses spoke, or about the healing properties of a plant she had read about, and what

Echo had to say was so interesting that Hera would lose track of time altogether. Hera cursed her, allowing her only to repeat the words she heard and never again to speak for herself. “I have been cheated enough by your chattering tongue,” Hera barked. “From now on you will only repeat what is spoken to you. You will never speak your mind again.” Echo replied mournfully the only words that she could: “Speak again.”

And so, when she saw Narcissus, Echo was unable to call out to him. Instead she followed the young man as he darted skilfully through the forest. Whenever he turned and spotted her, he smiled, and she smiled in return, but though he waited for her to call to him, she was silent. He set off again at a run, and just as Echo was about to lose him, he called out, “Who is following me?” And Echo responded, “Me, me, me.”

“I’ll stay here,” Narcissus called out to the mysterious voice, “and you come to me.” Again the voice of the nymph responded, “Come to me, come to me, come to me.”

“Fine, we’ll meet halfway,” said Narcissus. “Come.” And Echo responded, “Come.” As she saw Narcissus turn to face her, she raised her arms to embrace him – but being admired by so many had made Narcissus proud, and he rebuffed her as he had the others. “I would sooner die than let you touch me.” Echo’s voice rang out in a tearful whisper:

"Touch me, touch me, touch me."

Humiliated, the young nymph turned and ran, her footsteps resounding from the rocky cliffs above. She climbed inside a hole in an old tree and sat there, lamenting the young man who had rejected her before he had even heard what she had to say. For months she turned this over in her mind, wasting away from hunger. She stayed in the trunk of that tree until she was nothing but voice and bones. Her body turned to stone, sinking beyond the roots of the tree into the ground, and her voice drifted off by itself to the tops of the cliffs. She lived on only in the sound of each echo.

Narcissus, though, was still being followed by the rest of the nymphs – one by one he rejected them all. The scorned nymphs prayed: "Let him feel the pain he has made us feel – let him fall in love with one who rejects him."

Nemesis, the goddess of revenge, heard their prayers. One day, Narcissus came across a pool of water that was cleaner and clearer than any he had ever seen. He slumped down beside it and started to drink, but as he lowered his face towards the pool's surface, he caught sight of his own reflection. Narcissus never got up from the edge of that pool. He fell so deeply in love with his own reflection that he could not bear to be parted from it. For days he sat there, motionless, staring at himself in the water, not moving to eat or sleep. When he reached for his reflection, it vanished in the rippling water. He eventually wasted away, and in his place a single narcissus flower grew, leaning down to look on its own reflection for the rest of time.

PENTHEUS AND DIONYSUS

Back in the days when the old king Cadmus still ruled Thebes, the worship of the god Dionysos had been banned in the city. King Cadmus feared that too much worship of the god of wine, theatre and feasting would cause disorder.

When Cadmus became too old to be King of Thebes, he gave his throne to his grandson Pentheus. A man came to Thebes, dressed in the robes of a priest, and argued with Pentheus. He told the new king, in no uncertain terms, that he did not think it was right that the worship of Dionysus be banned. He threatened that Dionysus would punish King Pentheus if he did not allow his holy festivals to be celebrated in Thebes, but Pentheus ignored the man.

After dismissing him, Pentheus began to notice mysterious things happening in the city. He could hear the howling of wolves coming from the top of Mount Cithaeron, accompanied by singing and the beating of drums. And whenever he went to visit any of his friends' houses, Pentheus noticed that their wives and daughters were never there. When he asked where the women of the house had gone, his friends were evasive: "To the market," some said or, "To her bedroom to weave," replied others, though none of the men seemed sure. Pentheus grew suspicious of the mysterious priest. The king locked him in a prison cell, winding a chain around the door more tightly than usual, making sure that the man could not escape.

The sound of howling and singing did not stop on the mountain, and the next day one of Pentheus's servants arrived to tell him that he had seen the lock of the priest's cell spontaneously click open, and the chain slither like a snake to the ground. Pentheus called the prophet Tiresias, just as Oedipus would do many years later, to explain everything to him. "Your blood will pour

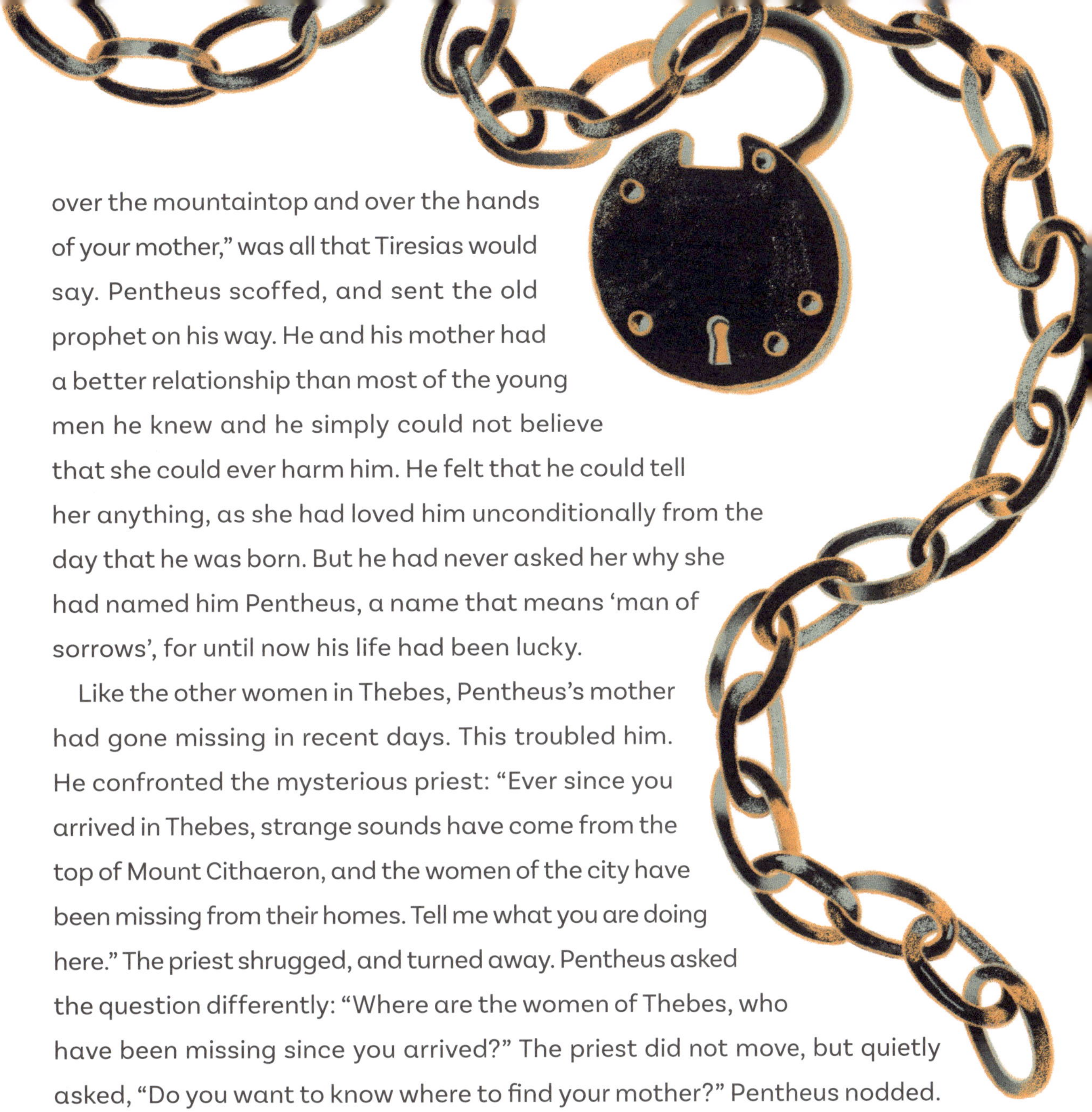

over the mountaintop and over the hands of your mother," was all that Tiresias would say. Pentheus scoffed, and sent the old prophet on his way. He and his mother had a better relationship than most of the young men he knew and he simply could not believe that she could ever harm him. He felt that he could tell her anything, as she had loved him unconditionally from the day that he was born. But he had never asked her why she had named him Pentheus, a name that means 'man of sorrows', for until now his life had been lucky.

Like the other women in Thebes, Pentheus's mother had gone missing in recent days. This troubled him. He confronted the mysterious priest: "Ever since you arrived in Thebes, strange sounds have come from the top of Mount Cithaeron, and the women of the city have been missing from their homes. Tell me what you are doing here." The priest shrugged, and turned away. Pentheus asked the question differently: "Where are the women of Thebes, who have been missing since you arrived?" The priest did not move, but quietly asked, "Do you want to know where to find your mother?" Pentheus nodded. The priest told him that she and the other women were on top of Mount Cithaeron, drinking wine, singing songs and worshipping the god Dionysos. The priest offered to take Pentheus to see what the women were doing. Pentheus agreed, thinking that he would catch those who were worshipping Dionysus against his ruling and put them in prison where they belonged.

Following the priest up to the top of the mountain, Pentheus climbed a tree, where he hid to watch the illegal religious festival. Soon, he spotted the women coming towards him, beating their drums and swaying their bodies to the beat. They began to sing, and then to howl like a pack of wolves. He spotted his mother, Agave, at the front of the group, and she seemed to be heading straight towards him. Suddenly, a sea of hands were grabbing at him, pulling him down from the tree and tearing off his tunic. One woman grabbed hold of each limb, while his mother held his head in both her hands. He called out to them to stop and look at what they were doing, but the women did not see King Pentheus. In his place, they saw a wild lion, roaring helplessly. It was like they were under the control of a cruel god. The priest looked on, unmoved. The women gave a howl louder than anything Pentheus had ever heard before and pulled hard. Pentheus was dead, his body torn to pieces by the women in their frenzy.

Agave put the head of Pentheus onto a stick and took it back down the mountain. She showed it proudly to her father Cadmus, thinking he would marvel at how she had hunted and killed a large mountain lion with her own hands. As she opened the door to her father's house, Agave began to revive from the spell Dionysos had put her under.

She looked again at the lion's head, thinking about how strange it was that its eyebrows and the shape of its nose reminded her of her son Pentheus. When Cadmus saw her arrive, he started to weep and demanded that she look again at the head she held in her hands. She recognised her own son this time, and shrieked, "What am I seeing?"

She broke down in tears, realising all too late that she had killed her own son. Behind her in her father's doorway, the priest took off his long, hooded cloak to reveal the youthful body of the god Dionysos. The god smiled – he had taught the royal family of Thebes a valuable lesson about what happens to those who refuse to worship the gods.

ACROSS THE SEA

As he told Little Owl the strange, sad stories of Thebes, Night Owl began to worry that he had kept his granddaughter away from home for too long. They set off back towards Athens. Almost as soon as they took off however, the two birds were hit by a sudden gust of wind. They were thrown around like leaves in a storm, first soaring high then dropping down almost to the ground. Night Owl closed his eyes and hoped the gods of the winds would allow the two of them to stay together.

The winds whistled through their feathers as they let themselves be carried by the storm. Little Owl could see nothing but dark waves, flowing backwards and forwards and crashing around her. They were flying over the sea (which the Greeks called 'thalassa', a word that makes the sound of the waves crashing on the shore). Night Owl thought fearfully of all the sailors who had set out across the ocean and never returned. Just below the horizon, three sharp metal spikes peered above the surface of the water. Night Owl recognised these as the spikes of Poseidon's trident. The sea was the realm of the sea god Poseidon, who lifted and lowered these waters twice a day, and tossed sailors and their ships from east to west. Little Owl was afraid of Poseidon.

THE TROJAN HORSE

Just across the sea from Thebes stood the city of Troy. Poseidon had built walls around it many years ago, back when Laomedon was king. Once he saw the walls and felt that his city was safe, King Laomedon saw no reason to bother honouring the sea god anymore. He felt powerful and secure, and this made him proud. Laomedon forgot that he owed his great fortune to the gods. He refused to thank Poseidon for the walls that he had built, and called him every name he could think of. He would pay the price.

The Trojans were at war with the Greeks. For ten years, the Greeks had been trying to enter the gates of Troy. Every morning they fought long and hard to take two steps towards the gate, and every afternoon they fought long and hard only to end up two steps further away from it. One day Odysseus, the cleverest Greek of them all, had an idea. He whispered into the ear of Epeius, who was in charge of the army, to order men into the forest to cut down trees and make planks. By day, the Greeks would continue their battle at the gates of Troy, and by night they would sneak out under cover of darkness and work on their secret weapon. After three days, the work was complete – an enormous wooden horse stood at the gates of Troy. Odysseus had chosen this shape because he knew that the horse was a symbol that was special to the Trojans.

Seeing such a huge wooden horse at their gates, he knew, would flatter them. But there was a secret hatch inside the horse's belly, and fifty Greeks were hidden inside, waiting for morning to come. Just before Odysseus himself climbed into the horse's belly, he took out a knife from his pocket and carved a message into the side of the horse:

τῆς εἰς οἶκον ἀνακομιδῆς Ἕλληνες Ἀθηνᾷ χαριστήριον

"The Greeks dedicate this horse to Athena to ensure their safe journey home."

When daybreak came, the Trojans put on their armour and returned to the gate to continue the battle, only to find that the Greek army had vanished and all that was left was a great wooden horse. They could not believe their luck. When they read the inscription, they assumed the Greeks had retreated and left the wooden horse as a peace offering. They could see no sign of the Greek ships or their tents, so they wheeled the gift inside their walls.

Meanwhile, the hidden Greeks could scarcely contain their excitement. But they all held their breath when they heard the voice of the Trojan priest Laocoon, warning the rest of the Trojans: "Beware the Greeks!" he boomed. "Even when they bring gifts!" The other Trojans laughed and told Laocoon that the Greeks had given up the fight. But just moments later, two huge serpents burst from the sea. One of them wrapped Laocoon in its scaly grip, and the other ripped his two sons from the shore. The Trojan saw this as a sign that Laocoon had made the gods angry, and ignored his warning... All except for a young woman named Helen, who remained unconvinced. To see whether there were any Greeks still around the city, she put on her best Greek accent and imitated the voices of their wives, calling for help as if they had been captured by Trojan soldiers.

She was so talented that the hidden Greeks were very nearly fooled. Anticlus even opened his mouth to answer – but Odysseus clamped his hand over it, and held his mouth tightly shut. Satisfied that the Greeks had truly departed, the Trojans took the wooden horse into their temple and planned a feast to celebrate their victory. When night fell, the Greeks slowly unhooked the hatch and, one by one, they slipped out of the horse's belly, taking their weapons and lighting their torches from the temple fires. While the Trojans slept, the Greeks swept through the city, destroying anyone and anything that stood in their way. By the next morning, the city of Troy belonged to the Greeks.

ODYSSEUS AND THE CYCLOPS

But Odysseus did not live happily ever after. On his way home from the war in Troy, Odysseus angered Poseidon. He was caught in a storm that swept him off course and blew his ships to the shore of a tiny island off the coast of Sicily. They moored their ships and set off to find out who lived there. As they walked up from the shoreline, they were surprised to find a cave with wine and fresh sheep's milk laid out, and they went inside. Moments later, a huge shadow was cast over the inside of the cave – someone, or something, was blocking the doorway. What the weary travellers didn't know was that this island was the land of the Cyclopes, and the home they had just barged into uninvited belonged to Polyphemus.

The men smelt him before they saw him, his breath a mixture of rotting flesh and sheep's milk. But Polyphemus did not seem to notice Odysseus and his companions as he ushered his flock of sheep into the cave, and with a flick of his index finger, he rolled the huge stone back over the doorway, closing himself and the men inside. The cave was thrown into darkness. Odysseus and his friends could not even see as far as their own fingertips.

In a frantic hush they started to pat the rocky walls, looking for another exit – but just then, they heard screams and the unmistakeable crunch of bones. The cyclops had eaten two of Odysseus's companions. Odysseus stopped himself from calling out to the monster, and held his breath until eventually the cyclops fell asleep.

The giant snored more noisily than the roar of the sea beating against the rocks at high tide. The men sat in silence, surrounded by sheep. They tried not to breathe too loudly, even when the smell of a thousand dead fish from the giant's breath spread throughout the cave. The next morning, the cyclops awoke, rolled back the stone and picked up one man in each fist as a snack. Then he called his sheep out to graze, and left the cave for the day. After he had taken a few deep breaths of the fresh air that flooded into the cave, Odysseus hatched a plan. He would not become a giant's dinner.

At the back of the cave, Odysseus found an enormous stick of olive wood. He chopped it in half, and then he and his friends whittled the end of it down to a point. Then they hid it under the piles of bones and sheepskins and old wine sacks that littered the floor of the cave. Their plan was simple: when the cyclops returned from grazing his sheep that evening, Odysseus and his companions would blind him with their new giant poker.

They sat… and waited. Eventually Polyphemus returned and called his flocks into the cave, but he did not settle down to sleep. Odysseus began to worry that the cyclops was suspicious of his plans, so he called out, his voice shaking: "Here, cyclops. Take this bowl of wine. We brought it with us from Troy especially for you." The cyclops peered curiously into the cave, looking down at the man holding up a bowl. Odysseys had quickly poured all the wine he and his companions had brought with them from the ship into one vessel. "Over here, cyclops," called Odysseus, luring the monster further into the cave. Polyphemus grabbed the wine greedily with one hand, took up another of Odysseus's companions in the other, and, holding his thighs like the bone of a chicken leg, devoured him. When he had finished, he used one of his bones as a toothpick and took another deep drink from the wine bowl, draining it dry. Odysseus had never seen anyone drink so much wine in one gulp.

"Tell me," Polyphemus's voice reverberated across the cave, "what is your name? I must know where this wine comes from. And give me more." Odysseus thought for a moment and then spoke. "My name is 'Nobody'. That is what my mother and father called me, and it is the name my friends use to get my attention." Odysseus tipped the last of the wine into the bowl. Again the cyclops drained it in one great gulp. "I will give you a present, Nobody, as you are such a dear guest. I will eat all of your friends one by one, and you, Nobody, I shall eat last of all."

As he was speaking these words, his enormous body slumped over and he fell into a deep, drunken snooze. Quickly, Odysseus ordered his friends to pick up the huge olive branch and place the tip of it into the fire so that it was hot and glowing. Moving as one, the men seized the olive branch, lifted it to their shoulders and hurled it straight into the cyclops's eye. He awoke with a scream that was louder than anything Odysseus had ever heard. Polyphemus rushed out of the cave, calling to his fellow Cyclopes: "Help, friends! Nobody has attacked me!" When the other Cyclopes heard his shout, they couldn't understand what Polyphemus meant. "Nobody has attacked you?" one replied. And another reassured him, "If Nobody has attacked you, then you are safe." They could not see what there was to worry about, and remained in their caves.

Now the men could escape. Odysseus took hold of the woolliest rams of the cyclops's flock and tied them together in groups of three using

willow branches. Then he ordered each of his men to cling on to the fluffy stomachs of the middle ram of every three, so that they could escape from the cave.

When the sun rose that morning, the rams wandered as usual down to the pasture, carrying with them Odysseus and his men. They passed Polyphemus, who felt around for humans but could only feel the wooly backs of sheep. When the rams had carried them far enough away from the cave, Odysseus and his men ran to their ships and climbed aboard, rowing away as fast as they could. Odysseus could not help but taunt the monster: "You, Polyphemus, dared to eat the guests who came to you looking for help. For that, Zeus has punished you!" That wasn't how the cyclops saw it at all. These men were not guests – they had broken into his home, eaten his food, blinded his eye and humiliated him in front of the other Cyclopes. But Odysseus was cruel, and proud of the hurt he had

caused to the cyclops. He continued, “If anyone asks you who blinded your one eye, cyclops, tell them it was Odysseus, the son of Laertes, on his way home from Troy to great Ithaca.”

Polyphemus shuddered to hear the name of the man who had blinded him. He had heard that name before, in a prophecy from many years ago. “Odysseus! I always knew I would lose my sight to a man with your name. But I had imagined him tall and strong. You, a weak little man, could not take my vision without first lulling me to sleep with dark wine. Let this be my last gift to you, Odysseus, my esteemed guest. Poseidon, my father, who rules the seas, if I am really your son, make it so that Odysseus will never again see his home in Ithaca. If he does find his way home, let him come too late and find his household in ruins.” With that, the cyclops tore a great rock from the side of a mountain and flung it into the sea, and Odysseus’ ship was rocked so violently by the waves that it nearly capsized. Odysseus and his friends had escaped for now, but Poseidon would not make the journey home easy for the men who had caused such hurt to his son.

KING MIDAS

As they sailed away, one of Odysseus' friends, Demodocus, told them a story while they rowed. Demodocus was a shy sort of person, who sometimes found it difficult to get a word in edgeways when large numbers of people were speaking – but people always listened when she told a tale. King Midas never intended to be cruel, Demodocus said. It was just one single, ill-advised wish that changed his life.

Midas was a king in Phrygia, even further east from Athens than Troy. One day, when he was walking through his rose gardens, he spotted an

old man snoring underneath one of his rose bushes. He stopped and woke the old man and asked him where he had come from. The man couldn't remember, though he knew that he was a friend of the god Dionysus. King Midas took the man straight to Dionysus, who was so happy to see him again that he promised to give King Midas whatever he wished for. Midas answered before he had given the offer any thought at all: "Let anything I touch turn to gold," he said.

Dionysus gladly granted his wish. Midas reached out to shake hands with the generous god, but Dionysus pulled his hand away and vanished into thin air. Midas was eager to try out his new power. He went out into his rose garden and touched the flowers on all of the rose plants, and one by one they turned into solid gold. He opened the door to go back inside, but as he did so, first the handle, then the whole door turned into gold.

Midas was enjoying his new gift so much that he did not notice the hunger that was growling in his stomach. He had been having so much fun he had missed dinner. He went to the kitchen for a snack, but all the ingredients that he touched turned to gold. Even the water in his cup turned to solid gold the minute that it touched his lips.

Three days went by, and Midas grew hungrier. On the fourth day he called Dionysus and asked him to take back his gift. Dionysus told King Midas that if he bathed in the river Pactolus, the gift would wash away with the water. Midas set off towards the river, but as he approached its banks he tumbled into the river. His golden touch washed away, leaving the banks yellow with gold. King Midas went on to become a good and grateful king, loved by all. Each flower, loaf and object he had touched remained golden.

As she finished telling her story, Demodocus looked at Odysseus and the other powerful men on the ship: she hoped that they were listening carefully to the story of thoughtless King Midas.

THE CITY OF ARGOS

Little Owl wondered out loud if Odysseus had ever made it home. Night Owl knew that she was scared. As the wind finally quietened and they flew over land again, he told her that the great hero had eventually returned home, but he and his friends had suffered at the hands of the angry Poseidon, and it had not been easy. Little Owl did not understand why Odysseus had been punished so harshly. "Poseidon punished him because he was arrogant," Night Owl said. "It was not enough for Odysseus to have escaped from the Cyclops: he chose to humiliate him too." Little Owl thought hard about Poseidon, who although equal to his brother Zeus, did not share the earth with all of his brothers and sisters. She felt a little sorry for the lonely sea god.

Eventually, Little Owl saw stone structures rising up in the distance – they were almost home. The city of Argos stood among fields so full of wheat that they looked like a blanket of gold. Here, the ground was so fertile that the farmers never slept.

For the last leg of their journey, Night Owl decided to tell Little Owl all the stories he could remember of the kings who used to rule in Argos. "But before I tell you," he said, "you need to understand something. Kings used to wish for all of their children to be princes. You see, humans assumed that women could not be leaders like men."

Little Owl narrowed her eyes. "What about Athena?" she replied angrily.

"Gods and goddesses were different," Night Owl said. "The gods always knew that the goddesses were equal in strength and intelligence, but the humans had not yet learnt this. That is what Athena would teach them."

PERSEUS AND MEDUSA

Acrisius, the King of Argos, was disappointed that he and his wife had not yet had a son. This was a problem because at the time, kingdoms only passed to princes, and not to princesses. He went to the Oracle at Delphi to ask her why he had no sons. The Oracle did not answer his question, saying only, "You will be undone by the son of your daughter." Acrisius did not like the sound of that, and what's more, it confused him because his only daughter, Danaë, had no children. Still, he trusted that the Oracle was telling the truth. He built his daughter a room of bronze in the courtyard of his palace: it had an open roof so that Danaë could enjoy the sunshine, but the walls were three times her height so that she could not escape. Acrisius believed that if he could keep his daughter locked away in there, she would not meet anyone, she would not fall in love and she would not have a child as the prophecy foretold.

One day, as Danaë was weaving in her bronze-walled room in the courtyard, clouds began to form above her. She saw the flash of Zeus's lightning bolt, and rain started to fall - not just any rain, but golden rain that clung to her body. Nine months later, Danaë gave birth to a son and named him Perseus. As soon as Acrisius found out that the child was a boy, he began to worry about what the Oracle had told him. He considered killing the child, but when Danaë told him about Zeus and the heavenly rain, Acrisius decided against this plan. Instead, he ordered Danaë and her young son to climb into a wooden chest, which his soldiers threw into the sea. After several seasick nights and days, the chest washed up on an island ruled by King Polydectes, whose name meant "one who welcomes many".

A fisherman named Dictys discovered Danaë and Perseus when he snagged his net on the corner of the wooden chest. Dictys took them straight home with him, and invited them to live in his house as if they were his own family. When Perseus was fully grown - and a competent fisherman himself - he began to suspect that King Polydectes felt something more than friendship towards his mother. The king was often found at the home of the humble fisherman, talking to Danaë.

One day, when Polydectes came to Dictys's house bearing a wreath as a gift for Danaë, Perseus confronted him. The king did not want rumours to spread about his feelings for Danaë, so he sent Perseus away on an impossible task, hoping that he would not return. He instructed him to bring back the head of the gorgon, Medusa. This monster had once been a beautiful young woman, but when Poseidon fell in love with her and found that she did not feel the same, he turned her into a monster with snakes for hair. He cursed her so that anyone who looked at her would be turned to stone. Perseus hadn't the least idea how to defeat such a creature, so he prayed to Athena for help. Athena appeared to him in full battle armour, telling him to find the Hesperides, the nymphs of the sunset. They were the only ones entrusted with the weapons necessary to kill Medusa. Though Perseus did not know where the Hesperides lived, he knew that the Graiai could tell him, so he set out to find them first.

The Graiai were three sisters as old as time itself. They shared between them one eye and one tooth that they each used in turn. Perseus walked for many days until he reached the vast darkness of their cave. As he blinked, waiting for his eyes to adjust, the three sisters passed their single eye between them so that they could each get a good look at the intruder. Seizing his chance, Perseus snatched the eye as it passed from hand to hand and put it into his pocket. The Graiai were enraged. "What do you want, stranger?" they cried, their voices harsh and throaty like a crow's.

“I need you to tell me where to find the Hesperi–” Perseus stopped speaking. The old women were shaking their heads – it seemed their minds were made up. “If you don’t tell me where to find the Hesperides,” threatened Perseus, “I will keep your eye in my pocket and you will never see again!” The old women grumbled and, without saying anything further, they spun on their heels all at the same time, and led him in single file out of the dark cave and towards the grove of the Hesperides.

As Perseus followed the Graiai towards the west, the sun began to sink and the world around him was bathed in the orange glow of sunset. The seven nymphs saw Perseus arrive, and it seemed as if they already knew why he had come. They opened their treasure boxes and gave Perseus winged

sandals from Hermes, the messenger god, a sword made of unbreakable diamond from Zeus, a polished shield from Athena, a helmet that made its wearer invisible, and a knapsack that they had woven themselves. Perseus thanked the Hesperides and paid close attention as they described the route to Medusa's cave.

After travelling for several days, Perseus noticed some strange statues appearing in the distance. As he approached, he saw that they were statues of men, only not the kind of statues any sculptor would design. Some recoiled in fear, while others were in kneeling positions with their heads turned back over their shoulders. He heard the hissing of snakes, and knew he had arrived at the Medusa's cave. He put on the helmet of invisibility so that she would not see him, and held the polished shield that belonged to Athena at an angle next to the doorway so that he could see the sleeping Medusa in its reflection. In a flash, he darted up to the Gorgon, who was snoozing in the corner. He sliced her head from her neck in a single swift motion, all the while keeping his gaze fixed on her reflection in the shield's polished surface. The snakes hissed and writhed on the severed head for a moment, then were still. Perseus grabbed the head and dropped it into the Hesperides' knapsack before fleeing on Hermes's winged sandals.

PERSEUS AND ANDROMEDA

On his way home, Perseus stopped in Aethiopia, a kingdom ruled by King Cepheus and Queen Cassiopeia. As he moored his ship and looked up, he was greeted by a terrible sight: a woman was chained to a rock hanging inches from the water. The woman was not flailing and tugging at her chains trying to escape, but was still like a statue, letting the waves lap at her ankles, with her face turned away from the water. Perseus approached a fisherman who was standing at the shore, packing fish into crates.

"That woman, who is she? And who has tied her to this rock at the mercy of the sea?" he asked. He was amazed at the strength and the courage of the woman silently remaining still above the waves. Before the fisherman could answer, the water started to ripple around her ankles and splash against the shore, growing until the waves were so violent that Perseus was afraid that the woman would drown.

A huge dragon-like creature rose up from the water, gnashing its teeth, and stretching its tail across the whole harbour. The fisherman answered Perseus's question: "Andromeda. Daughter of King Cepheus and Queen Cassiopeia. Her mother boasted that she was prettier than the nymphs of the sea, and Posei-". Here the fisherman broke off as the sea serpent's tail lifted, and fell with an almighty crash, sending salt water hurtling up against the rocks.

"Poseidon," he continued, "was enraged at the suggestion that anyone could be more beautiful than those nymphs of the sea. So-"The fisherman dodged to the left to avoid a thick clump of seaweed that the monster hurled past his ear. "So, he sent this... monster."

Perseus did not understand what this had to do with Andromeda, but the fisherman continued: "The King went to visit the Oracle to find out how he could get rid of the monster. But what he heard made him wish he had not asked. You see," the servant went on, "the Oracle told the King that Poseidon's anger would not be calmed until the King and Queen had given their daughter to the monster. And as you can see, that is what they did."

Perseus lifted his head and looked across at the young woman, who still showed no fear even though the monster was inches from her ankles. He tore open the bag that the Hesperides had woven for him and pulled out the head of the Gorgon, grasping it by a handful of snakes. Medusa's eyes had not lost their power, even in death. He ran down the coastline and up onto the cliff where, face-to-face with the monster, he held up Medusa's severed head. The monster raised its head and looked straight into the eyes of Medusa the Gorgon. Its eyes were the first to turn to white marble, then its neck began to lose its colour and soon its whole body was enveloped in cold stone. Perseus released Andromeda from her chains and there, under the stony gaze of the monstrous statue, he asked her to marry him, and she agreed.

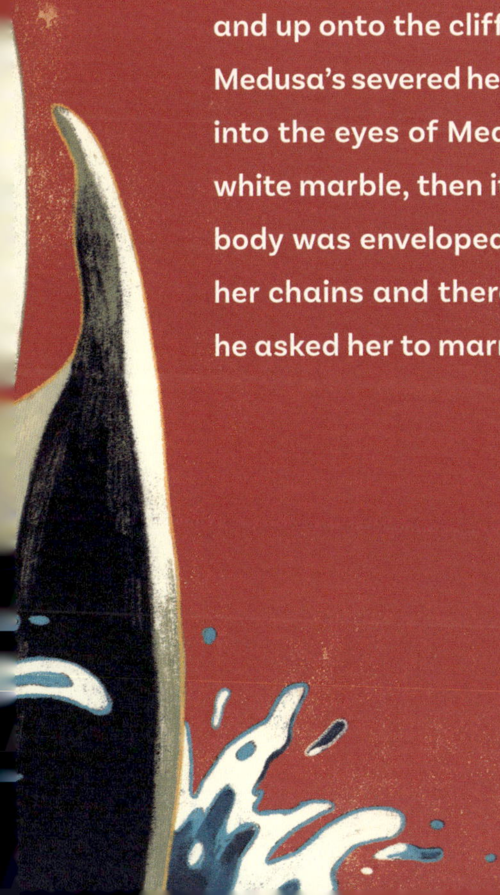

Perseus eventually returned to Argos to present the head of Medusa to King Polydectes and see his mother again, but when he arrived, she was nowhere to be found. He searched all over the city, until finally he came to a small temple and discovered his mother locked inside. King Polydectes was standing guard over his prisoner with some of his soldiers. It had been years since Perseus had left, and King Polydectes was so surprised to see Perseus alive that he could do nothing but stare. Perseus seized his chance, reaching into his knapsack and pulling out the head of Medusa once again.

The king and his soldiers gazed at the head in amazement – and in that same moment, they were all turned to stone. Perseus released his mother from her prison, and gave the kingdom of Argos to her and the fisherman Dictys, who she had always loved.

But Perseus could not escape from the prophecy that he would kill his grandfather, King Acrisius. Hearing that Perseus had returned to Argos,

Acrisius fled, and sought refuge further north in Thessaly. Perseus knew nothing of the prophecy and could not understand why his grandfather would leave, so he set off to find him. When he arrived, he found the whole town in the heat of an athletic tournament. Perseus signed himself up for the discus-throwing competition. When his turn came, he picked up the flat stone circle, drew his shoulders around his body and released the discus with all the force he could muster. It was a brilliant throw: the discus headed in a straight line down the field, outstripping all of the other competitors by almost half the length of the stadium. But just as it crossed the furthest marker, the disc began to change direction, whirling around to the east and – Perseus realised, to his horror – straight towards the crowd. He tried to call out and warn them, but it was too late. The discus struck his grandfather with such force that it killed him instantly. There are some prophecies that simply cannot be avoided.

THE LABOURS OF HERACLES

Heracles, too, was a king of Argos who found himself at the mercy of a dark and murderous prophecy. The goddess Hera had hated Heracles since his birth, for although Heracles's father was her husband Zeus, his mother was a human woman named Alcmene. When he was born, he was given the name Heracles – or "glory to Hera" – in the hopes that this might calm the goddess. It did no such thing, and one day Hera put Heracles under a spell that drove him to kill his own wife and children. Upon awakening from the spell, Heracles realised in horror what he had done and went to the temple of Apollo for guidance. Apollo told Heracles to go to Mycenae and serve King Eurystheus for twelve years. If he did this, Apollo promised, he would be rewarded with an immortal life.

Heracles was not sure why he would want to live forever now that his wife and his children were gone, but he knew better than to argue with the gods. He went straight to Mycenae and knelt at the feet of Eurystheus, promising to do whatever the king asked of him. Eurystheus was thrilled by such a loyal follower, and was quick to dream up all the dangerous tasks and trials he could think of.

First, the King told Heracles to slay the enormous Nemean lion. The lion was huge, but it also had some suspiciously magical features. Heracles thought that he had met his match when the lion's fur proved to be impenetrable – neither his arrows nor his sword could puncture it. In the end he had to enter the lion's cave and strangle it with his bare hands.

Next, Eurystheus sent Heracles to Lerna to kill the Hydra, a sea serpent with nine venomous heads. The Hydra was even more fearsome than the lion. Every time Heracles chopped off one of its nine heads, two more sprouted in its place, so that very quickly it had seventy-two heads, all of them hissing and spitting venom. He summoned his friend Iolaus to help, and together they used a burning branch to cauterise the bleeding stumps of the Hydra's neck, so that new heads could not grow. But when Heracles and his friend returned to the palace of Eurystheus, the King refused to recognise their triumph, since the labour had not been completed by Heracles alone.

For his next pair of tasks, Eurystheus ordered Heracles to bring back two animals alive. The first was the sacred stag of Ceryneia, with golden antlers and golden hooves. Heracles followed the stag for a whole year, until finally he tracked it down, wounded it with an arrow and carried it over his shoulders back to Mycenae. The second creature was the Erymanthian boar, which he caught in a net after chasing it through knee-deep snow for days.

When he had seen both of these animals safely stabled within his kingdom, Eurystheus set Heracles another challenge: to clean the stables of Augeas. Augeas owned thousands of cows – so many that despite hundreds of workers cleaning the stables all night and all day, they looked as though they had never been cleaned at all. Heracles found Augeas and offered to clean the stables before the sun set, in return for one tenth of Augeas's cattle. Augeas agreed, amused by such a ridiculous promise.

But Heracles had a plan. He made a deal with the two rivers that flowed on either side of Augeas's farm. The rivers would leave their normal routes and flow straight through Augeas's stables. The rivers agreed, and they rushed through the stables with such force that nothing remained of the muck, hay and leftover barley that had littered the floors. Again, Eurystheus refused to count this challenge among Heracles's ten, as he felt it was the rivers, not Heracles, that had really cleaned the stables.

Eurystheus then ordered Heracles to confront the birds who had taken refuge in a lake near Stymphalus for fear of being eaten by wolves. When he arrived at the shore, Heracles found that these were no ordinary birds. They had bronze beaks and talons, and there were so many of these terrifying birds that he could not even see the lake. The crops in the surrounding fields had been pecked away, and all the trees' branches bent down to the ground under the weight of thousands of birds. As Heracles approached the lake, Athena presented him with a golden rattle made by Hephaistos. Heracles shook it, and its earsplitting sound made the birds fly up into the air. They did not return.

For his seventh task, Eurystheus asked Heracles to bring the Cretan bull back to Mycenae. Poseidon had sent the Cretan bull to King Minos of Crete as a symbol of his leadership, expecting King Minos to sacrifice the creature in his honour. But when he saw the bull, the King decided that it was too beautiful to be killed. He led the glimmering white beast to his herds and chose another bull to be Poseidon's sacrifice instead. Poseidon did not like being given second best, and in order to punish King Minos and his family, he made the King's wife Pasiphae burn with love for the white bull. Every night Pasiphae would sneak down to the fields and sit with the bull, stroking its white skin in the dark. Eventually, Pasiphae gave birth to a terrifying creature that was half-man and half-bull, which was called the Minotaur. Heracles found the bull, wrestled it to the ground, tied it up and brought it back with ease.

Next, Eurystheus ordered Heracles to go to Thrace, a land famous for horsemanship, to fetch the mares of King Diomedes. These bloodthirsty horses ate only human flesh, and though the thought of them frightened Heracles, he did as he was asked. Heracles killed Diomedes and flung his body to the mares, who chewed and chomped on his flesh as if he were made of grass. Happy and full, they stood quietly as Heracles put on their bridles, and brought them back to Eurystheus.

Eurystheus considered his next request, and ordered Heracles to fetch a belt that belonged to the famous Queen Hippolyta, as a gift for his daughter.

Queen Hippolyta ruled the Amazons, a race of fierce warrior women. When Heracles eventually arrived at the land of the Amazons, he found the queen, explained his situation and asked whether he could take her belt as a gift for Eurystheus's daughter. To his surprise, Hippolyta agreed, but as she was taking off the belt to give it to Heracles, Hera appeared.

The goddess felt that Heracles was having much too easy a time given what he had done to his family, and vowed to make things harder for him. She disguised herself as an Amazon and sent whispers of distrust through the women. She told them that the Queen of the Amazons must have been tricked into giving her belt to a mysterious stranger. They encircled Hippolyta with their double-sided axes drawn by their sides.

When Heracles saw this, he thought that Hippolyta - not Hera - had tricked him. He dodged all of their weapons, killed the Amazonian queen and raced back to his ship as quickly as he could, belt in hand.

For his tenth labour, Eurystheus commanded Heracles to fetch the red oxen belonging to Geryon, a giant with three bodies, six hands, six feet and a huge pair of wings, who lived on the western island of Erytheia.

Heracles had to cross the desert of Libya to get there. He made it half way across before he felt nearly overcome with exhaustion and cursed the sun for its never-ending heat. Losing his temper, he shot an arrow at the sun. To his pleasant surprise, the god of the sun Helios lent Heracles his chariot so that he could fly the rest of the way to Erytheia. The first thing he saw on the island was a large snarling dog with two heads - but Heracles despatched it with his club, and did so again when Eurytion the herdsman came to see what had caught the dog's attention.

When he heard the cries of Eurytion and the howling of his dog, Geryon leapt up and armed himself for battle, putting on three helmets and holding a shield in each ginormous pair of hands. Heracles did not wait for the three-bodied monster to find him, and instead turned around and carefully drew one of his poisoned arrows from the quiver that hung over his shoulder. He shot Geryon straight in the middle of his forehead, and the giant fell to his three sets of knees, his three necks bending towards the ground. Heracles took the staff out of the herdsman's hand and herded the oxen back towards Eurystheus's palace. Hera thought to herself - again - that Heracles was having too easy a time. She sent a gadfly to bite the red oxen and send them running in different directions. It took Heracles almost a whole year to herd them back together again. As soon as he had gathered together all of the oxen and moved towards Mycenae, Hera sent a flood that filled the river so high that the oxen could not get over it. Heracles piled stones

into the river until it was shallow enough for the animals to cross. Imagine the look on Heracles's face when Eurystheus announced that the reason he wanted the oxen in the first place was so that he could give them as a gift to Hera!

Because he refused to accept two of Heracles's previous labours, Eurystheus gave him two more: to fetch the golden apples of the Hesperides, and to bring Cerebus, the three-headed dog, back from Hades. As far as Heracles knew, only the Titan Atlas could take the golden apples from the garden of the Hesperides. After the Titans were defeated by the gods, Atlas had been condemned by Zeus to hold the weight of the sky on his shoulders for all eternity.

Eventually, Heracles found Atlas. His shoulders were so worn out from holding up the sky that he almost dropped it in relief when Heracles offered to take over for a few moments while Atlas fetched the golden apples for him. When Atlas returned with the apples, he offered to take them to Eurystheus himself. "To save you the journey," he said. Heracles sensed it was a trick, but he worried that Atlas might be angry if he did not agree. Instead, he tricked him in return, saying, "Of course, Atlas, you must take the apples to Eurystheus. A long-legged giant like you will cross the ocean much more quickly than me." Atlas thought that his ruse had worked. "But before you go," Heracles continued, "take hold of the sky for one moment, so that I can arrange my cloak over my shoulders." Atlas put the apples down and took the weight of the sky from Heracles. While he concentrated on lifting the world back onto his shoulders, Heracles slipped away, taking the golden apples with him.

Eurystheus was amazed when he saw Heracles coming towards him with a sack full of apples over his shoulder. The hero had done it again!

Next, Heracles set off into the Underworld, where he met Hades and asked for permission to take Cerebus. The three-headed dog snored from each of its dark, wet noses as Heracles and Hades spoke. Hades agreed to let Heracles take Cerebus – who, after all, was not a particularly good guard dog given he had not woken up when Heracles came in – but only if Heracles could get the dog to go with him without using any weapons. Heracles was one of those people who dogs just seemed to listen to. He clicked his teeth, called Cerebus by name, and the three-headed dog trotted out of the Underworld behind him.

Heracles brought the dog to Eurystheus's palace. But despite asking for one, the king was in fact scared of dogs, and eventually Heracles found him cowering at the bottom of a large jar. Eurystheus begged him to take Cerebus back to the Underworld, and promised that if Heracles returned the dog he would not force him to perform any more labours. Heracles looked at the dog, whose six large brown eyes had never stopped looking for their master Hades, and agreed to take it back to its home.

When he had completed all twelve labours, Eursytheus agreed that Heracles had been punished enough. But Heracles, who had no family to return to, missed the adventure and danger that he had grown used to. Eventually, he joined Jason and the Argonauts and sailed off into the distance in search of the golden fleece.

THE UNDERWORLD

"Heracles had to do all that," Little Owl said, "because of something he did under a spell that Hera cast on him – something he did not mean to do?"

Night Owl nodded solemnly. "He did do it, and that's what matters," he said.

The owls had barely left Argos when Little Owl suddenly spotted something moving below them. It gleamed white, even in the darkness. It was another owl. As they approached. Night Owl called out to the white owl: "Excuse me." he said, "Hello?"

The owl did not seem to hear. He was the largest owl that either of them had ever seen. They hovered beside him until, finally, he turned to look at them. White Owl, for that was his name, spluttered, startled, and from his mouth he spat a seed covered in a deep red flesh.

"What's that?" whispered Little Owl. "A pomegranate seed," Night Owl explained. Curious, they followed White Owl as he swooped down, disappearing under the long grass.

When he approached the ground, hurtling at speed, they were baffled and fluttered their wings to slow down – but suddenly, the ground below them gave way to a crack, small at first then wider.

As if they were being pulled by an invisible rope, the owls squeezed through into the ground itself. Little Owl closed her eyes and stuck close behind Night Owl, clutching at his tail feathers with her beak. They soared downwards through endless twists and turns, in darkness blacker than anything they had ever known before. Soon they reached a dimly lit cave where White Owl stopped suddenly, perching on what looked like the stern of a small wooden boat.

Frogs of all shapes and sizes covered almost every inch of land in this strange place. Little Owl's eyes widened until they were the size of dinner plates. White Owl beckoned to them to approach the rickety old boat. Looking back, Night Owl and Little Owl saw that the crack had closed up behind them. They had no choice. Nervously, they settled in the front seat, and suddenly noticed a creature sitting at the other end. He looked almost human, except that his eyes blazed like a blue fire, and the long stick clasped in his fingers looked like it had grown from his gnarled hand. White Owl opened his beak and dropped a single gold coin into the creature's lap. He opened his eyes and lowered his long stick into the water below. Suddenly, and with a lurch of fear, Night Owl recognised him.

This was Charon, the ferryman who guided souls to the Underworld.

The frogs started to sing a croaky song as the boat pulled away from the shore and sailed down the dark river.

In a silence that seemed to go on forever, the owls sat petrified as Charon thrust his long stick into the water and drew it out again, inching the boat forwards. He rowed them past an open field, where happy souls lay out in the sunshine eating plates of fruit and talking to each other about art and poetry. They also rowed past cages with iron bars full of grey, faded souls. Little Owl only caught a glimpse of these because Night Owl covered her eyes with his feathers. Eventually, the boat came to a stop with a gentle bump, and Night Owl's voice returned.

"We... we would like to go home now please," he said to White Owl.

"Home?" White Owl almost laughed. "But you are home! The souls of all living things come home to the Underworld eventually."

Night Owl gulped, loudly. He looked at Little Owl, who was trembling a little, though she fluffed up her feathers and tried to hide it. "Home to Athens," Night Owl said, "and to Athena."

White Owl paused, amused. He spat another pomegranate seed from his beak, and began to tell his favourite story.

DEMETER AND PERSEPHONE

One of Zeus's daughters was called Persephone, and her mother was Demeter, the goddess of the harvest. One day, Persephone was picking flowers by the side of a clear pool of water, pulling them up by their stems and stuffing them into her pockets until she could barely fit in another petal. She reached for one last flower, grasped it between her thumb and forefinger and pulled gently, but the flower would not move from the ground. She pulled harder, and felt the flower lean towards her, but still it wouldn't budge. With one last enormous tug, it came out of the ground, pulling out a great chunk of earth with it.

Persephone knelt down to inspect this curiously strong flower. It looked fairly ordinary she thought, but as she held it, the flower seemed to wither away. Its petals turned brown and shrivelled up. Its stem became so weak that the flower slumped over, leaning towards the hole in the ground. She felt an icy grip close around her wrists, and in an instant she was dragged down through the hole and into the Underworld.

When Persephone did not return home that night, her mother did not know what to do. She called out for her daughter, and when she received no answer, she ran all over the earth in search of her. She cried so many tears that there was no water left in all of the world for farmers to water their crops. There was no harvest that year, and many of the humans grew so hungry that they thought they might not survive. Eventually the Sun, who had been watching the suffering that Demeter's grief caused to the humans, took pity on the goddess, and told her what had happened. This was no accident of fate, Demeter thought, but a kidnapping. Hades, the god of the Underworld, had found a way to the world of the living through the crack in the ground and had stolen her child.

Demeter went to visit Zeus on Mount Olympus straight away. "Our daughter has been kidnapped by Hades. What are you going to do to save her?" Zeus wasn't sure. Hades was his brother, and the two had equal power, except that while Zeus's powers controlled the land of the living, his brother's controlled the land of the dead.

It wasn't long before Zeus too heard the cries of the hungry humans from the earth below and reluctantly offered a solution. "You can bring our daughter back," Zeus said, "as long as she has not eaten a single mouthful of food from the Underworld." Demeter frowned. She needed to reach Persephone before she got too hungry.

As Demeter entered the Underworld, she felt her daughter's presence. Amid all of the gloom and death that hung in the air she noticed patches of fresh corn growing, and she smiled as she realised that she must have passed her own powers of raising crops on to her daughter. Suddenly, she saw her. Persephone ran towards her mother with tears in her eyes and began to tell her everything that had happened. But Demeter only wanted to hear one thing. "Please tell me you haven't eaten anything since you have been here," she said.

Persephone swore that she had not, but Demeter knew that she was lying. "It was only seven pomegranate seeds," she confessed eventually. "How could I have known that something so small could do so much harm?"

Demeter was inconsolable. They made their way to the centre of the Underworld and stood at the doorway to the palace of Hades. There, Demeter begged and pleaded with Hades to release Persephone.

She begged him to make an exception for his own flesh and blood, but Hades had got used to the life that Persephone brought to the land of the dead.

Eventually, unable to agree but both afraid to anger Zeus, Demeter and Hades reached a compromise. Persephone would spend half of the year in the land of the living with her mother, and the other half in the Underworld with Hades. Demeter had no choice but to accept this, and eventually all of the earth followed suit. The six months that Persephone spent in the land of the living with her mother were bright and warm, with bees buzzing loudly around flowers that stretched up towards the sky. Then, when the time came for Persephone to return to the Underworld, the flowers withered and died, and a blanket of darkness and a cold chill fell over the earth. This is the story of why the seasons change.

ALCESTIS

Although Persephone was not allowed to spend all of her days in the land of the living, she was able to help another woman do so instead.

Alcestis loved her husband Admetus more than she had ever thought possible, and neither of them could imagine life without the other. On the night that they were married, Admetus had promised to say a special prayer to Artemis, the goddess of wild animals and hunting. With everything else that was going on that day, Admetus forgot to make the prayer, and Artemis punished him by hiding a writhing mass of poisonous snakes in the bed he shared with Alcestis. But when she threw back the covers that night to get into bed, Alcestis did not panic. Instead she called out to Apollo to help them.

Apollo was embarrassed. After all, it was his sister Artemis who had put the snakes there, and she had clearly forgotten that he and Admetus were old friends. To make up for this, Apollo promised Admetus that he would be allowed to live beyond the moment of his death if, when that moment came, someone else would give up their own life and die in his place. Admetus gladly accepted his gift, but when fate decided it was time for Admetus's death, none of his companions offered to give their life in exchange for his. Admetus began to wonder whether he had been naïve to think that Apollo's gift would be of any use to him at all.

At the very last moment, Alcestis flung open the doors to his room, and offered her own life. As soon as she had spoken these words, Alcestis dropped to the floor. Her body was placed in a tomb, and her soul began to make its way down to the Underworld, while Admetus lived on.

The first person that Alcestis met in the Underworld was Persephone, who listened to her story with a mixture of admiration and confusion. She struggled to understand how anyone could value another's life over their own. She objected to Alcestis's arrival in the Underworld before her time, and vowed to return Alcestis to the land of the living. Alcestis agreed, but only after she had convinced Hades not to take Admetus's life in return for hers. Persephone led Alcestis up through the tunnel that guided them back to the earth and settled her on Charon's ferry. Though Persephone could not board the ferry herself for another three months, Alcestis was taken back to the land of the living, and given many more years to spend with the husband whom she loved more than life itself. Her sacrifice had been worth it.

THE LAND OF THE LIVING

Little Owl was relieved. White Owl's stories had given her hope that she and Night Owl would be able to make it out of the Underworld after all. The two Athenian owls fluttered their wings and carried on further into the darkness, which was strangely peaceful now that they had left the singing frogs behind. The spirits did not seem to notice them, and carried on with their own business as if they had never really died at all.

Night Owl saw something glinting in the distance as if it were reflecting a mysterious light. He beckoned for Little Owl to follow him as he went to take a closer look, hoping that it might be a way back to the land of the living. Both of them desperately wanted to go home to Athens. When they drew near enough to see, they were surprised to find a golden owl standing on a pedestal in a corner. Night Owl slowly approached the statue. He recognised the owl instantly, even though when he had known her, she had not been made of gold. It was Wise Owl. Night Owl called out to Little Owl to come closer. "What is it?" she said, not sure whether to be worried or excited.

"Little Owl," he said, sounding more serious than Little Owl had ever heard him, as if something heavy was sitting at the back of his throat. "Meet Wise Owl." He paused. "Your grandmother."

As Night Owl spoke, something deep inside the golden statue stirred. Although she did not move, Little Owl could tell the golden owl had something to say. "My grandmother?" Little Owl sounded surprised. 'But how... What happened to you?" One golden feather stirred.

"Did King Midas touch you?" the Night Owl asked, his voice becoming thin as if at any moment he might not be able to speak. "That was the winter when there were no mice to eat in Athens, and you flew down to Phrygia," Night Owl said. "Is that why I never saw you again?" There was a noise like the clang of freshly-forged metal, and Little Owl saw that Wise Owl was nodding. She watched as her grandfather rested his head on her grandmother's golden wing. All of this time, he had wondered and waited. Now he knew the truth – his partner had been turned to gold by King Midas's fatal touch. Night Owl wanted to stay in the Underworld forever with his long-lost mate, but he knew that Little Owl still had too much living left to do. As much as it hurt him to even think of leaving Wise Owl behind, they had to go back to Athens.

Raising one stiff, metallic wing, Wise Old pointed. In the distance was a faint light. There was another crack – the way out! Night Owl took one last, long look at Wise Owl. Then he turned, gathered up Little Owl with his wing, and swept her up into the air. With a heavy heart, the two owls flew across the river, and started the long journey back up through a winding tunnel and out into the land of the living. Even though he wanted to, Night Owl did not look back.

Eventually, they saw the fires of Athens rising over the horizon. It felt like they had left a lifetime ago. Night Owl settled on the top of the Parthenon. Little Owl nestled beside him. They were silent for a long time, but eventually Night Owl spoke. "Have you ever wondered how the owls arrived in Athens?" he asked.

"No," she said. "It feels like we have always belonged here." Little Owl yawned,

her beak gaping open as if she might swallow the sun rising behind the trees on the Areopagus.

"It didn't look like this when your grandmother and I first arrived," Night Owl said. "Back then, there was just a single olive tree. It didn't look strong, but it had been planted by the goddess Athena, and so it could easily hold a whole parliament of owls. For the first time since we had left the pine trees on Mount Pelion, we felt truly at home. And that was it. Even when Athens was just a single olive tree, this was where we felt we belonged. We have been the companions of that goddess ever since."

The sun had nearly risen, and Night Owl could see that Little Owl was exhausted. As they settled in to sleep away the day, he wanted to explain one last thing to her – about how Athens became the Athens she knew.

CECROPIA

Long ago, before the Athens we know today, this land was called Cecropia. It was named after its founder, King Cecrops, who was part-man and part-snake. Cecrops was quickly turning his small piece of land into mud by ploughing it with heavy-footed oxen, and the gods were not happy about it. They wanted to build a city on Cecrops's land and to name it after one of them, though first they had to decide who. A fight broke out among the gods and goddesses, and Athena and Poseidon overpowered all of the others before coming face-to-face with each other. They drew their weapons, but Zeus stopped them, worried about what might happen to the human world if they could not reconcile. He proposed a gift-giving competition rather than a war. King Cecrops would decide which gift was the best, and whoever had given it would become the patron of the new city and give it their name.

All of the gods and goddesses gathered on top of Mount Olympus to see what would happen. Poseidon went first. He lifted his trident high and plunged it deep into the ground, causing a spring of water to jet out of the rock. Cecrops was thrilled, for the people of this new city (Poseidonia, he thought they might call it), would always have plenty of water for drinking and washing and growing their crops. But when Cecrops went down to the spring to taste the water, he found that it was salty like the sea and realised that it would be of no use. Next, it was Athena's turn to present her gift. She took what looked like the stone of an olive from her pocket and placed it in the ground. The gods and goddesses waited in silence for a moment, and then the branches of an olive tree suddenly sprouted up from the soil. Its leaves were beautiful and delicate, its trunk thick and strong. Cecrops liked this gift much more than Poseidon's saltwater spring because it would give the citizens olives, oil and wood for their fires. King Cecrops declared Athena the winner, and the city was named Athens after the generous goddess. The name remains to this day.

THE FURIES

For a long time after it was founded, the city of Athens had no courts, so citizens took the law into their own hands. One citizen would punish another who had done them wrong however they saw fit. But as the Athenians learnt, whether something is right or wrong depends on who you ask. This system could not go on. Eventually something happened that was so serious Athena herself stepped in.

King Agamemnon was killed by his wife Clytemnestra. His crime was that he had killed their daughter Iphigenia. But Agamemnon – if he had had the chance to explain – would have told the story differently. He had sacrificed Iphigenia to the gods in exchange for a wind to blow his ship and crew safely home. He would have said there was no other choice.

When Agamemnon and Clytemnestra's son Orestes arrived home he was determined to avenge his father's death. He decided to kill his mother. As she fell dead to the ground, Orestes felt a chill run up his spine: the Furies were coming from the Underworld. It wasn't just humans who sought revenge in Athens, but goddesses too. To kill him, they thought, would be fair, since he had killed his mother. But Athena had had enough of all this.

This wasn't the city that Athena had dreamt of. There had to be a process for deciding what was right or wrong. She decreed that each time a crime was committed, twelve citizens would hear both sides of the story. They would vote to decide whether the accused was guilty or innocent. Athena made a deal with the Furies. She offered them a special place as goddesses of Athens alongside her, on the condition that instead of seeking revenge, they sought kindness. She gave them a new name, 'The Bringers of Kindness' and waited to see how all of this new 'justice' would turn out.

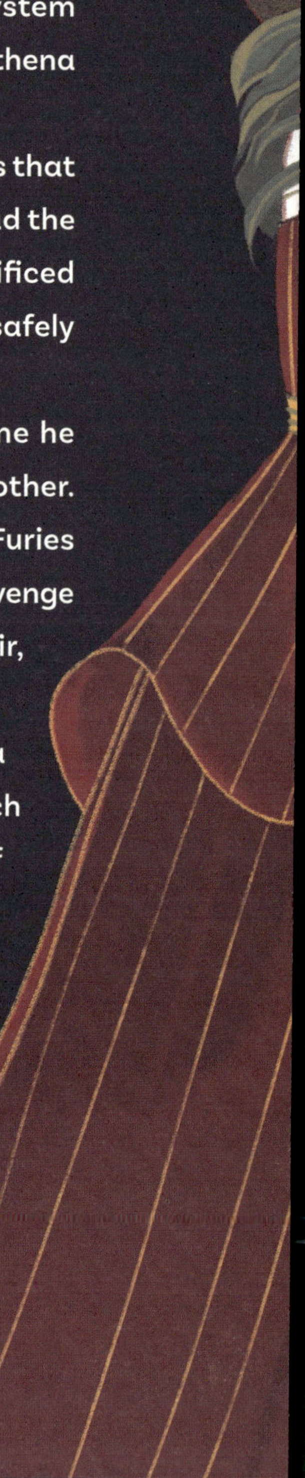

THE MINOTAUR

Athena might have been able to stop the Athenians from taking revenge amongst themselves, but not even Athena could stop others from taking revenge on the Athenians. All cities have their share of sadness, and for the Athenians, it was the Minotaur. Androgeos, the son of King Minos and Queen Pasiphae, had come from Crete to compete in the games at Athens. He defeated his opponents in every event, but his good luck ran out, and he was murdered by a jealous competitor. Androgeos's father Minos was distraught. He rounded up his best soldiers and led them to Athens where they fought and defeated the Athenians. He had avenged his son, but there was something more King Minos wanted from the Athenians, and they were in no position to refuse.

Many years ago, his wife had been struck with a strange love for a beautiful white bull, and had given birth to a baby which was half-man and half-bull – the Minotaur. As the baby grew older, he became more and more ferocious, and he began to develop a taste for human flesh. King Minos wrote to Daedalus, the most skilled inventor in his kingdom, and asked him to build a home for the Minotaur inside his palace, from which the beast could not escape. Daedalus built a labyrinth so intricately patterned that even the inventor himself could not find his way out.

Though he was now contained, the Minotaur still needed to be fed. Minos requested that the Athenians send seven young men and seven young women to Knossos every nine years, to be kept in the city and fed to the hungry Minotaur one by one.

Twenty-seven years passed in this way, and every nine years the Athenians chose seven young men and seven young women and sent them away to Knossos. When it was time for the third group of people to be sent, a young man named Theseus volunteered to go, planning to kill the Minotaur and save future Athenians from this fate. He took the place of one of the men in the boat and promised his father that his ship would return, hoisting a white sail if he was successful and a black one if he was not. All of the young people on the boat had their armour and weapons removed as soon as they arrived in Knossos, but Theseus managed to hide an extra sword deep in the folds of his tunic. Luckily, he did not have to carry out this task alone because Ariadne, the daughter of King Minos, offered him a ball of thread from her loom so that he could lay a trail to find his way out of the labyrinth. She made him promise that if he survived, he would return to Athens and take her with him, and he agreed.

Theseus tied one end of the thread to the doorpost and held the roll of thread out behind him, leaving a trail in the darkness. He strode further and further into the labyrinth, following the sounds of the great monstrous snores that shook the walls. With every twist and every turn in the labyrinth, Theseus held his breath. The beast could be around any corner – he would come across him soon enough.

Finally, he found the Minotaur asleep in the very heart of the labyrinth.

The air was sour with the smell of rotten flesh, and skulls and bones of young Athenians littered the floor. Theseus tried to tiptoe quietly around the sleeping beast, but as he drew the sword from his tunic, the monster awoke with a mighty roar and whirled around to grab him between his sharp teeth. The Minotaur was quick, but Theseus was quicker, and holding the bull by one enormous horn, he cut off the monster's head with a swift stroke. Theseus found the thread with his hands in the dark and followed it back to the door, where he set the remaining young Athenians free as he had promised. But as they triumphantly arrived at the shoreline, Athena appeared to Theseus and gave him stern orders: "Leave now, and don't look back." Theseus thought of his promise to Ariadne, his eyes brimming with tears, but he knew he had to obey the goddess's command.

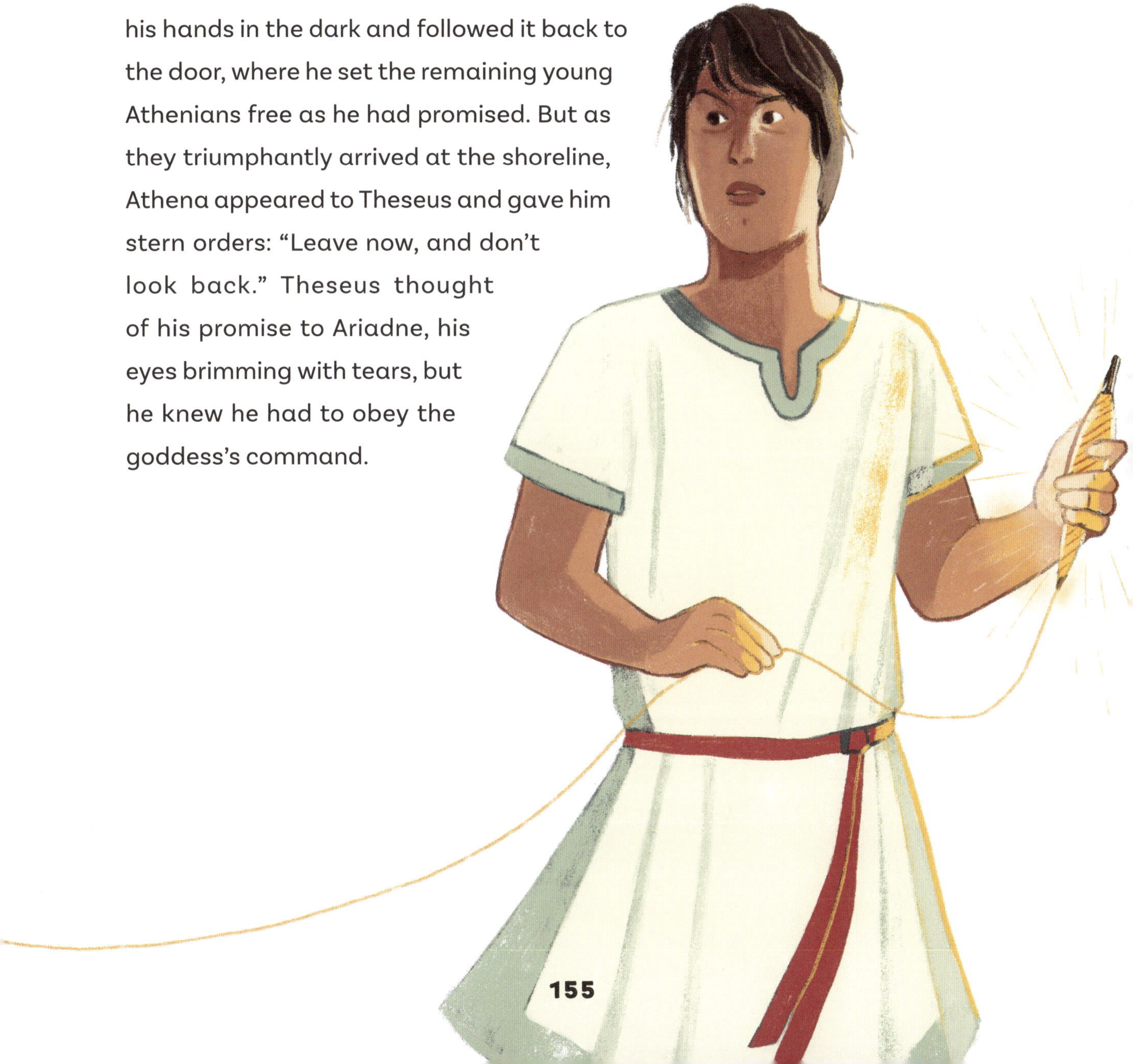

Theseus boarded the ship and sat quietly, thinking sadly of Ariadne who he had left behind. He was so deep in thought that he forgot to change the black sail on the ship to a white one. Soon the ship approached Athens, and Theseus's father could clearly make out the black sails flapping against the mast. Assuming that this meant the certain death of his son, Theseus's father collapsed in grief and fell to his death in the waters below.

DAEDALUS AND ICARUS

In order to prevent the inventor Daedalus from divulging the secrets of the labyrinth he had built, King Minos had him locked in a tower. The tower was well-equipped, and Daedalus and his young son Icarus had enough to eat, but they were desperate to be free. The tower was too high for them to climb down, and even if they could, they would not have been able to sail away from the island because King Minos kept a careful watch on ships leaving the port.

Eventually, Daedalus came up with a plan – he would make pairs of wings so that they could fly to freedom and begin their lives again. He gathered the feathers of the various types of birds that roosted by his window, and glued them together with wax. When he had finished, Daedalus found that by beating the wings up and down like the wings of a bird, he could raise himself up above the floor of the tower. He set about teaching his son this skill. One day, when he thought they had both had enough practice, he attached one pair of wings to his own arms and one pair to his son's.

Before they left the tower, Daedalus had one very important piece of advice for his son: "Don't fly too close to the heat of the sun". He was scared for his son's safety, but knew they had no choice if they wanted to be free. They opened the window, flapped their wings and glided out together over the water. After they had passed over three or four islands, Icarus began to drift upwards. He felt giddy at the thought of how high he was flying, and carried on rising up towards the sun until he felt a hot drop of wax fall onto his ankle. Panicked, Icarus tried to fly back down, away from the scorching rays, but it was too late.

His melting wings fell apart, and he plunged into the sea below and drowned. His father hovered over the waves, searching for his son. When he saw the feathers floating on the surface of the water, he knew Icarus was dead. Daedalus cried for weeks and weeks. He cried so much that the people who lived nearby named the ocean 'Icaria', because they were so used to hearing Daedalus calling out his son's name across its waves.

HOME AT LAST

Night Owl was quiet for a moment. He thought about how grateful he was that owls flew in the dark, cool night. Of all the things he hoped that his stories would teach Little Owl, there was one thing he cared about most. He thought of Wise Owl. He thought about the day he had been forced to leave his home on Mount Pelion where they had shared their lives. Every time the owls had arrived in a new place, they had told each other stories to explain how things came to be as they were – and now Little Owl knew those stories too.

There were other things he hoped that these stories would teach Little Owl: not to be arrogant, to keep her promises, to be kind of others and to stand up against injustice. But more than anything else, he wanted Little Owl to know that stories can turn even the most unlikely places into homes. He turned to Little Owl to tell her this, but she had fallen asleep. He sighed and turned his head to look down over Athens, the city he had come to call home. The humans were stirring. Soon, it would be time for him to sleep away the day until the sun sank again.

Little Owl would never forget how her grandfather had gifted her the myths that explained her place in the world. She would tell the stories herself, in her own way, and each time she told them the stories would change. A myth never stays in one place for too long. Night Owl's eyes closed. He could sleep peacefully knowing that no matter where Little Owl flew, the stories of the owls would always guide her home.

AFTERWORD
ATHENA AND THE OWLS

No one really knows why Athena chose the little owl (*Athene noctua*) to be her special companion. Both Athena and the owl were said in ancient literature to be keenly intelligent, with bright eyes. They were also said to have a special relationship with warfare (seeing an owl on the battlefield was taken by Athenians as an omen of victory).

Whatever the reason, Athena claimed the owl as her own very early in her history, and the owl therefore also became associated with the city of Athens. Athenian coins from the 6th century BCE onwards show the owl, and the bird was a frequent feature of Athenian vases, particularly those given as prizes at games and used during festivals. Even when the Greek goddess Athena became the Roman goddess Minerva, her association with owls remained. In Ovid's poem *The Metamorphoses*, the crow complains about the fact that her spot as the goddess' sacred bird has been given to the owl.

There has always been a connection between owls and stories. For the Romans, this connection was dangerous: placing an owl's feather next to a sleeping person, the Romans thought, could make them tell all their secrets. Birds telling stories appear frequently in ancient literature, and the little owl, as the wisest of them all, makes the perfect companion to Athena, the goddess of war, craft and wisdom, and the key to all the ancient stories of Athens.

ABOUT THE AUTHOR AND ILLUSTRATOR

MARCHELLA WARD is a classicist and spends her days chasing myths and legends from the ancient world through the libraries of the University of Oxford, UK. Her research interests are less in what the ancient world was really like and more in how the ancient world set the terms for what the modern world could be. This is her first book for children.

SANDER BERG is a Swedish illustrator. His artwork focuses on colour, text and contemporary digital artwork and he loves the visual storytelling aspect of drawing. *A Journey Through Greek Myths* is his first children's book.